Immigrants' Rights
After 9/11

POINT | COUNTERPOINT

Affirmative Action

Amateur Athletics

American Military Policy

Animal Rights

Capital Punishment

DNA Evidence

Election Reform

The FCC and Regulating Indecency

Fetal Rights

Freedom of Speech

Gay Rights

Gun Control

Immigrants' Rights After 9/11

Immigration Policy

Legalizing Marijuana

Mandatory Military Service

Media Bias

Mental Health Reform

Miranda Rights

Open Government

Physician-Assisted Suicide

Policing the Internet

Protecting Ideas

Religion in Public Schools

Rights of Students

The Right to Privacy

Search and Seizure

Smoking Bans

Stem Cell Research and Cloning

Tort Reform

Trial of Juveniles as Adults

The War on Terror

Welfare Reform

Immigrants' Rights
After 9/11

Wendy E. Biddle, J.D.

SERIES CONSULTING EDITOR
Alan Marzilli, M.A., J.D.

CHELSEA HOUSE
PUBLISHERS
An Imprint of Infobase Publishing

Chelsea House
An imprint of Infobase Publishing
132 West 31st Street
New York NY 10001

ISBN-10: 0-7910-8682-8
ISBN-13: 978-0-7910-8682-7

Library of Congress Cataloging-in-Publication Data

Biddle, Wendy.
  Immigrants' rights after 9/11 / Wendy Biddle.
     p. cm. — (Point/counterpoint)
  Includes bibliographical references and index.
  ISBN 0-7910-8682-8 (hardcover)
  1. Immigrants—Civil rights—United States. 2. United States—Emigration and immigration—Government policy. I. Title. II. Title: Immigrant's rights after nine eleven.
  JV6456.R53 2006
  323.3'29120973—dc22   2006017147

Series design by Keith Trego
Cover design by Takeshi Takahashi

Printed in the United States of America

Bang Hermitage 10 9 8 7 6 5 4 3 2 1

This book is printed on acid-free paper.

CONTENTS

Foreword
Alan Marzilli, M.A., J.D.
Washington, D.C.

The debates presented in POINT/COUNTERPOINT are among the most interesting and controversial in contemporary American society, but studying them is more than an academic activity. They affect every citizen; they are the issues that today's leaders debate and tomorrow's will decide. The reader may one day play a central role in resolving them.

Why study both sides of the debate? It's possible that the reader will not yet have formed any opinion at all on the subject of this volume—but this is unlikely. It is more likely that the reader will already hold an opinion, probably a strong one, and very probably one formed without full exposure to the arguments of the other side. It is rare to hear an argument presented in a balanced way, and it is easy to form an opinion on too little information; these books will help to fill in the informational gaps that can never be avoided. More important, though, is the practical function of the series: Skillful argumentation requires a thorough knowledge of *both* sides—though there are seldom only two, and only by knowing what an opponent is likely to assert can one form an articulate response.

Perhaps more important is that listening to the other side sometimes helps one to see an opponent's arguments in a more human way. For example, Sister Helen Prejean, one of the nation's most visible opponents of capital punishment, has been deeply affected by her interactions with the families of murder victims. Seeing the families' grief and pain, she understands much better why people support the death penalty, and she is able to carry out her advocacy with a greater sensitivity to the needs and beliefs of those who do not agree with her. Her relativism, in turn, lends credibility to her work. Dismissing the other side of the argument as totally without merit can be too easy—it is far more useful to understand the nature of the controversy and the reasons *why* the issue defies resolution.

The most controversial issues of all are often those that center on a constitutional right. The Bill of Rights—the first ten amendments to the U.S. Constitution—spells out some of the most fundamental rights that distinguish the governmental system of the United States from those that allow fewer (or other) freedoms. But the sparsely worded document is open to interpretation, and clauses of only a few words are often at the heart of national debates. The Bill of Rights was meant to protect individual liberties; but the needs of some individuals clash with those of society as a whole, and when this happens someone has to decide where to draw the line. Thus the Constitution becomes a battleground between the rights of individuals to do as they please and the responsibility of the government to protect its citizens. The First Amendment's guarantee of "freedom of speech," for example, leads to a number of difficult questions. Some forms of expression, such as burning an American flag, lead to public outrage—but nevertheless are said to be protected by the First Amendment. Other types of expression that most people find objectionable, such as sexually explicit material involving children, are not protected because they are considered harmful. The question is not only where to draw the line, but how to do this without infringing on the personal liberties on which the United States was built.

The Bill of Rights raises many other questions about individual rights and the societal "good." Is a prayer before a high school football game an "establishment of religion" prohibited by the First Amendment? Does the Second Amendment's promise of "the right to bear arms" include concealed handguns? Is stopping and frisking someone standing on a corner known to be frequented by drug dealers a form of "unreasonable search and seizure" in violation of the Fourth Amendment? Although the nine-member U.S. Supreme Court has the ultimate authority in interpreting the Constitution, its answers do not always satisfy the public. When a group of nine people—sometimes by a five-to-four vote—makes a decision that affects the lives of hundreds of millions, public outcry can be expected. And the composition of the Court does change over time, so even a landmark decision is not guaranteed to stand forever. The limits of constitutional protection are always in flux.

These issues make headlines, divide courts, and decide elections. They are the questions most worthy of national debate, and this series aims to cover them as thoroughly as possible. Each volume sets out some of the key arguments surrounding a particular issue, even some views that most people consider extreme or radical—but presents a balanced perspective on the issue. Excerpts from the relevant laws and judicial opinions and references to central concepts, source material, and advocacy groups help the reader to explore the issues even further and to read "the letter of the law" just as the legislatures and the courts have established it.

It may seem that some debates—such as those over capital punishment and abortion, debates with a strong moral component— will never be resolved. But American history offers numerous examples of controversies that once seemed insurmountable but now are effectively settled, even if only on the surface. Abolitionists met with widespread resistance to their efforts to end slavery, and the controversy over that issue threatened to cleave the nation in two; but today public debate over the merits of slavery would be unthinkable, though racial inequalities still plague the nation. Similarly unthinkable at one time was suffrage for women and minorities, but this is now a matter of course. Distributing information about contraception once was a crime. Societies change, and attitudes change, and new questions of social justice are raised constantly while the old ones fade into irrelevancy.

Whatever the root of the controversy, the books in POINT/ COUNTERPOINT seek to explain to the reader the origins of the debate, the current state of the law, and the arguments on both sides. The goal of the series is to inform the reader about the issues facing not only American politicians, but all of the nation's citizens, and to encourage the reader to become more actively involved in resolving these debates, as a voter, a concerned citizen, a journalist, an activist, or an elected official. Democracy is based on education, and every voice counts—so every opinion must be an informed one.

———————•————————•————————•———————

U.S. citizens enjoy many protections in criminal investigations and prosecutions; however, the ongoing War on Terror has led the federal government to adopt more restrictive measures for dealing with non-citizens, both those who have immigrated to the U.S. and those who have been detained by U.S. forces. This volume examines some of the controversies related to these measures, which go so far as to monitor the communications between detainees and their attorneys. This practice gained national attention when a lawyer was convicted for helping the "blind sheikh" involved in the 1993 World Trade Center bombing communicate messages to his supporters. The government also takes measures that would never be considered acceptable treatment of citizens—such as holding non-citizens indefinitely without charging them with crimes. While the federal government has justified such measures in the name of national security, civil libertarians maintain that these measures violate basic human rights. What is particularly troubling to critics is that these tactics are being used outside of the public eye. With a national cable network devoted to live television coverage of trials and extensive coverage in other media outlets, most trials are more open than ever to the public. However, deportation hearings for "special interest" aliens—purportedly with ties to terrorism—are closed to the public, the media, and even family members. While the government argues that secrecy prevents communication among terrorists, civil libertarians are concerned that the closure of these hearings will cover civil rights violations.

Civil Liberties for Immigrants

Anser Mahmood was arrested in October 2001 for an expired visa. Originally from Pakistan, he was living in Bayonne, New Jersey, and working as a truck driver. The FBI went to Mahmood's home looking for Mahmood's brother-in-law; instead, they took Mahmood into custody, on the charge that he overextended his business stay. After they arrested Mahmood, the FBI assured him that he would be home the next day.

Mahmood did not return home the next day. Instead, he was shackled and beaten with other Muslim men picked up during the FBI's other sweeps in the area. Mahmood spent four months in jail, in solitary confinement, in the Metropolitan Detention Center located in Brooklyn, New York. He was not allowed to speak with his family or his attorney for at least two weeks.

Six months after he was first arrested, Mahmood was finally charged with using an invalid Social Security card. Mahmood pled guilty and was deported to Pakistan with the requirement that he never set foot in the United States again.[1]

Immigrants in the United States

The United States admits between 700,000 and 900,000 legal immigrants per year, plus millions of long-term and short-term visitors (tourists, business travelers, students, and workers). It is much easier for immigrants to become citizens in the United States than in virtually any other country—in 2005 alone, more than 600,000 people began the year as foreigners and ended it as Americans.

Generous immigration and asylum laws, coupled with a democratic respect for diversity of lifestyles and viewpoints, have long distinguished the United States from any other country in the world. Many people dream of immigrating to this country and making a better life for themselves. The United States operates on a democracy premised on "faith that government officials are forthcoming and honest, and faith that informed citizens will arrive at logical conclusions."[2]

When a person from another country enters the United States, he either does it legally or illegally. When a person enters legally, he has a visa that grants him permission to enter the United States. There are many different kinds of visas, including tourist visas, student visas, and work visas. All visas expire after a certain amount of time, and if an immigrant stays past that proscribed time, he is considered to be in the United States illegally. An immigrant can also enter the United States illegally by not having proper documentation, having false documentation, or avoiding border checkpoints.

The United States responded vigorously to the terrorist attacks on September 11, 2001, the results of which included the destruction of the World Trade Center in New York City and severe damage to a wing of the Pentagon, as well as the deaths of thousands of people. Since that time, in addition to taking military action, President George W. Bush and his administration, the U.S. Justice Department, and the U.S. Congress have

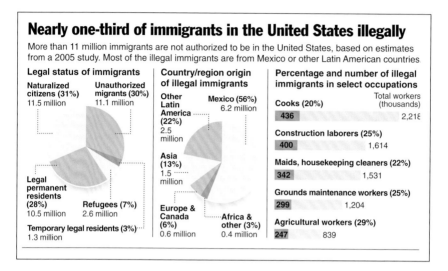

Nearly one-third of immigrants in the United States illegally

More than 11 million immigrants are not authorized to be in the United States, based on estimates from a 2005 study. Most of the illegal immigrants are from Mexico or other Latin American countries.

Legal status of immigrants

Naturalized citizens (31%) 11.5 million

Unauthorized migrants (30%) 11.1 million

Legal permanent residents (28%) 10.5 million

Refugees (7%) 2.6 million

Temporary legal residents (3%) 1.3 million

Country/region origin of illegal immigrants

Mexico (56%) 6.2 million

Other Latin America (22%) 2.5 million

Asia (13%) 1.5 million

Europe & Canada (6%) 0.6 million

Africa & other (3%) 0.4 million

Percentage and number of illegal immigrants in select occupations

Total workers (thousands)

Cooks (20%) 436 — 2,218

Construction laborers (25%) 400 — 1,614

Maids, housekeeping cleaners (22%) 342 — 1,531

Grounds maintenance workers (25%) 299 — 1,204

Agricultural workers (29%) 247 — 839

A 2005 study reported that more than 11 million immigrants are not authorized to be in the United States. As shown above, these 11 million people make up nearly one-third of the immigrants currently residing in the United States.

enacted a series of Executive Orders, regulations, and laws that have altered Americans' civil liberties, as well as the checks and balances that are essential to the structure of the democratic government.

The Constitution

The Constitution of the United States separates the federal government into three distinct branches and provides a system of checks and balances that prevents any one branch of government from accumulating excessive power. The system of checks and balances and the separation of powers are based upon the theory that one branch of government should not be able to overpower the others. "Separation of powers" means that the government is divided into three branches, with each branch having specific powers. Not only does each branch of government have its own dominion, each also has certain powers that help to keep the other branches "in check."

The first 10 amendments to the Constitution are called the Bill of Rights. The Bill of Rights is not a declaration of the rights citizens owe one another. It is a declaration of the rights of individuals, rights that prevent the federal government from having too much control and from interfering in the lives of its citizens. The rights guaranteed by the Fourth, Fifth, Sixth and Eighth Amendments relate to the criminal justice process. They protect against abusive exercises of the power to arrest, search, prosecute, and punish for crime. The First, Second, Third, and Seventh Amendments protect rights outside of the criminal justice process. The Ninth Amendment states that the rights of U.S. citizens are not limited only to those detailed in the Bill of Rights. The Tenth Amendment allows government functions not claimed by the federal government to be fulfilled by state governments.

The Fourteenth Amendment, ratified in 1868, equipped the Supreme Court with a constitutional mechanism that could be used to convert the guarantees of the Bill of Rights into rights that are also protected against deprivation by the state governments. In short, the Fourteenth Amendment extended the due process clause of the Fifth Amendment so that it applied to state governments as well as the Federal government. The Fourteenth Amendment forbids the states from depriving any person of life, liberty, or property without providing them the process due under the law.

The individual rights established by the U.S. Constitution do not uniquely protect U.S. citizens. Instead, nearly all of the individual rights protected by the Constitution are rights of "persons," not "citizens."[3] It follows that immigrants in the United States enjoy substantial constitutional protections.[4] The Supreme Court of the United States, the highest court in the nation, has consistently held that even those who are present illegally in the United States are "persons" under the Due Process clause of the Fifth Amendment, dispelling the notion that these constitutional guarantees extend only to citizens and legal immigrants.[6] Following the terrorist attacks of September 11, 2001, however, there have been many concerns that immigrants have not been able to rely on the judiciary to guarantee that their rights are not sacrificed in the name of national security.

The Constitution precludes states from drawing virtually any distinction between citizens and noncitizens, except when necessary to preserve political functions of the state. Under the Equal Protection Clause of the Fourteenth Amendment, states can no more discriminate against noncitizens than they can against citizens. The federal government, on the other hand, has the power to discriminate against noncitizens. According to the doctrine of congressional plenary power over immigration, when the plenary power applies, Congress may subject immigrants to substantive immigration laws that would otherwise violate constitutional principles. This broad power lets Congress regularly make rules "that would be unacceptable if applied to citizens."[6] Congress could, for example, enact a discriminatory deportation law requiring the removal of all legal immigrants from Egypt, Saudi Arabia, and Iraq. Deportation is the act of forcing an immigrant to leave the United States.

The USA PATRIOT Act

The USA PATRIOT Act,[7] which was signed into law two months after the September 11 attacks, was intended to detect and disrupt terrorist activities within and outside of the United States.[8] The act included several provisions modifying immigration policy:

- Section 402 authorized a tripling of the number of border patrol personnel, customs personnel, and immigration inspectors along the U.S. northern border, plus an additional $100 million to improve monitoring technology along the northern border.

- Section 403 granted the Department of Homeland Security and State Department personnel access to the FBI's NCIC-III (database of criminals) and the Wanted Persons File in order to check the criminal history of visa applicants.

- Section 411 broadened the grounds for exclusion of immigrants with ties to terrorist organizations. It authorized the exclusion of the spouses and children of immigrants who have engaged in activities linking them to terrorist organizations and made inadmissible any alien who is determined to have been associated with or who supported any terrorist

Sunset Provisions to the Patriot Act

Under the original Patriot Act, several provisions authorizing new kinds of surveillance were set to expire at the end of 2005. Congress thoroughly reviewed the provisions before renewing them in 2006. To David Cole, writer for *The Nation* magazine, however, these were not even the most objectionable provisions:

> Among the most troubling provisions not sunsetted, or monitorialy expiring, are those on immigration. Those provisions authorize the government to deny entry to foreigners because of speech rather than actions, to deport even permanent residents who innocently supported disfavored political groups and to lock up foreign nationals without charges.
>
> The government has used the PATRIOT Act's immigration provisions to revoke the visa of Tariq Ramadan, a Swiss professor and a leading thinker on Islam's relation to modernity. Ramadan, one of the first prominent Muslim scholars to condemn the 9/11 attacks, had been offered a prestigious chair at Notre Dame. Yet the government revoked his visa on the basis of something he said, without ever informing him of what it was. More recently, the government denied a visa to Dora Maria Tellez, a Nicaraguan invited to teach at Harvard, solely because of her association with the Sandinistas in the 1980s.

Source: David Cole, *The Nation*, May 30, 2005 issue.

organization. Exclusion prevents a person who seeks entry to the United States from entering the country. Contrast this with deportation or removal, which describes the compulsory expulsion of a person who is no longer legally allowed to remain in the United States.

- Section 412 directed the Department of Homeland Security (DHS) to detain and remove any alien certified to be engaged in terrorist activities. It authorized the secretary of the DHS to certify any alien as a terrorist if there are reasonable grounds to believe that he or she is affiliated with a designated terrorist organization or is engaged in terrorist activities. It restricted judicial review of such detention to habeas corpus proceedings.

- Section 413 authorized the secretary of state to share with foreign governments information in the State Department's visa-lookout database and—under certain circumstances—information regarding individual immigrants. The secretary of state may do so for the purpose of combating terrorism.

In summary, the immigration provisions of the USA PATRIOT Act (also known as the Patriot Act) restrict what immigrants can do and how they are treated within the borders of the United States with the goal of curtailing terrorism.

Military Tribunals

A military tribunal is a special court run by the military, and it is used to try extraordinary cases, usually during wartime. In November 2001, President Bush issued an executive order authorizing military tribunals for foreigners accused of terrorism.

When the Bush administration first announced they would use military tribunals to try noncitizens accused of aiding terror groups, it had significant bipartisan and public support. But it also drew criticism from both sides of Congress, human rights groups, and foreign governments, who said that the tribunals fell short of national and international standards of due process for the accused.

How are military tribunals different from civilian courts?

Military tribunals are different from civilian courts in many ways. The crimes for which one can be tried in a military tribunal are defined by the Defense Department, whereas in a civilian court, the crimes are defined by Congress and state legislatures in legal statutes.[9] The jury in a military tribunal is made up of three to seven military officers, whereas in a civilian court, a jury is made up of 12 citizens, randomly chosen by voter or licensed-driver lists. The attorney for the accused, in a civilian court, reviews and can eliminate potential jurors; no such option is available in military tribunals. The rules of evidence used in a military tribunal are more strict in national security concerns than in civilian court, but there are rules in both courts governing the suppression and admittance of evidence. Convictions in a military tribunal are made by a two-thirds vote of the panel; in a civilian court, convictions require a unanimous agreement of all 12 jurors.

Has the government used civilian courts instead of tribunals to try terrorists?

The U.S. government used civilian courts to prosecute the perpetrators of the 1993 World Trade Center bombing, the conspirators in a failed plot involving New York City tunnels, and those responsible for the 1998 bombings of two U.S. embassies in Africa. Partly in response to the initial outcry over military tribunals, the Justice Department opted to use federal courts to try the first person charged in the September 11 conspiracy: Zacarias Moussawi, a French citizen and the "twentieth hijacker." Moussawi was convicted in 2006.

Military Tribunals

President Bush authorized the use of military tribunals through an executive order (Congress did not vote on it) on November 13, 2001. Military tribunals apply only to noncitizens (they can be legal residents of the United States, but not citizens). According to the president, the purpose of the tribunals is to help more swiftly fight the War on Terror by speeding up the process to convict terrorists.

CIVILIAN CRIMINAL TRIAL DUE PROCESS GUARANTEES

- Defendant can have either a trial by jury or a bench trial with a judge as the decision maker if he or she chooses.
- The jury must all agree unanimously on guilt or acquittal.
- Illegally seized evidence is excluded from consideration by the jury (Exclusionary Rule).
- Defendant can appeal automatically to the appeals court.
- Defendant must have access to all the evidence against him or her.
- Defendants has a right to a lawyer.
- Defendants is innocent until proven guilty.
- Defendant does not have to testify.
- Double Jeopardy applies —cannot be charged for the same crime twice (same crime, same victim, same time, same place, same manner, etc.).
- Rules of evidence apply.

MILITARY TRIBUNALS DUE PROCESS GUARANTEES

- Applies only to noncitizens who have allegedly performed, aided, abetted, or conspired to commit international terrorism.
- Military officers judge the case, and military officers are the jury (3–7 appointed members will hear the case).
- Unanimous verdicts are not required—only 2/3 of the military commissioners (jury) are needed to convict.
- The rules of evidence do not apply (e.g., hearsay is allowed).
- Illegally seized evidence (in violation of the Fourth Amendment) can be admitted as evidence (it would be excluded in a civilian trial).
- Defendants that are convicted cannot appeal to a civilian judge, but they can ask for a "review" from a three-member panel selected by the Secretary of Defense. The Secretary of Defense then decides whether to perform the review or not.
- Evidence can be withheld from defendants and their lawyer whether classified as secret or not.
- Defendants have a right to a lawyer (unless designated as an "enemy combatant" by the president).
- Defendants are innocent until proven guilty.
- Defendant does not have to testify.
- Double Jeopardy applies—cannot be charged for the same crime twice (same crime, same victim, same time, same place, same manner, etc.).

Who would be subject to these tribunals?

Essentially, any non-U.S. citizen who the government alleges is a terrorist or an accomplice to terrorism could be tried in a military tribunal rather than a civilian court. According to President George W. Bush's executive order, the military tribunals would apply to any foreign individual who is a member of al Qaeda, has engaged in or aided acts of terrorism against the United States, or has knowingly harbored such a person.

Why is the government setting up these military tribunals?

White House officials maintained that military tribunals would allow the government to try suspected terrorists quickly, efficiently, and without jeopardizing public safety, classified information, or intelligence-gathering methods and operations. The officials also said that the tribunals would protect American jurors, judges, and witnesses from the potential dangers of trying accused terrorists.

According to some Bush administration officials, the government is reluctant to try captured terrorists—especially leaders of the Taliban and the al Qaeda terrorist network—in conventional U.S. courts, where their trials and appeals could take years and turn into spectacles. In December 2001 congressional testimony, Attorney General John Ashcroft asked: "Are we supposed to read [alleged terrorists] their Miranda rights, hire a flamboyant defense lawyer, bring them back to the U.S. to create a new cable network of Osama TV or what have you?"[10] Under the March 2002 guidelines, press coverage of most tribunal proceedings was permitted, although cameras were banned from courtrooms. Bush administration officials also worried that some terrorists might go free if they had to be proven guilty beyond a reasonable doubt, as is required in the civilian court system.

Immigration Services and Enforcement

The U.S. Immigration and Naturalization Service (INS) is still the most recognized name when it comes to the government agency that handles legal and illegal immigration and naturalization. Following September 11, however, certain government agencies were reorganized, including the INS, which ceased to exist as such on March 1, 2003. On that date, its former function were transferred to three new agencies. The U.S. Citizenship and Immigration Services (USCIS) took over the functions relating to permanent residence, naturalization, asylum, and others. U.S. Immigration and Customs Enforcement (ICE) took over the investigation and enforcement roles, including deportation and intelligence. The Border Patrol and INS inspectors, originally part of the INS, were absorbed in to U.S. Customs and Border Protection (CBP). This book will use INS when referring to events that took place before March 1, 2003, and the other terms when referring to actions taken by those agencies after they came into existence.

Summary

There are many immigrants in the United States, and even more who wish to enter. To handle the flow of legal immigration, the United States has passed many laws to govern the process. Because the terrorists who committed the 9/11 attacks were foreigners, the president and Congress have enacted new measures to ensure that would-be criminals and terrorists are not allowed into the country. Many Americans, however, feel that new policies have unfairly restricted the liberties of people who come to the United States for legitimate reasons.

One example of new government actions is the controversial use of military tribunals. They are seen as an attempt by the U.S. government to hide information from the general public, and to convict and punish suspects with less evidence than would be considered reasonable in a civilian court—thereby increasing the chance that the defendant might be guilty.

The Right to an Attorney Is Being Ignored for Immigrants

The Sixth Amendment to the U.S. Constitution provides that every person accused of a crime has the right to an attorney. The attorney-client privilege, "one of the most venerable of the evidentiary privileges in Western jurisprudence," dates from more than two millennia ago, to ancient Rome.[1] Indeed, in Roman times there was no waiver of the privilege, based in part on the custom that the lawyer must not betray confidences. An attorney's testimony on behalf of his client was viewed as "completely valueless," because he would have had a strong motive to lie and was therefore not credible. If the attorney testified against his client, he was considered disreputable, and thus not to be believed. The Romans' approach was based on the notion that preserving the confidence and trust among family members and "quasi-family" relations was more important than the "correct settlement of controversies" or the punishment of wrongdoers.[2]

The rule protecting attorney-client communications remains in the American legal system; it is a privilege held by the client, limited and protected by statutory or common law rather than by the Constitution.[3] The rationale for the privileges, as laid out in eighteenth-century England, also has persisted through time in American jurisprudence. In 1888, Justice Fuller wrote for the Supreme Court:

> The rule which places the seal of secrecy upon communications between client and attorney is founded upon the necessity, in the interest and administration of justice, of the aid of persons having knowledge of the law and skilled in its practice, which assistance can only be safely and readily availed of when free from the consequences or the apprehension of disclosure.[4]

But the privilege, Justice Fuller admonishes, is the client's alone, "and if the client has voluntarily waived the privilege, it cannot be insisted on to close the mouth of the attorney."[5] Similarly, in a more recent, well-known case, *Upjohn Co. v. United States*, Justice Rehnquist reasoned that the privilege encourages "full and frank communications" between counselor and client, promoting "broader public interests in the observance of law and administration of justice."[6]

Attorney-client confidentiality is necessary for the assistance of counsel to be effective.

Hearkening back to the early days of the Republic, the U.S. Supreme Court, during the height of the Civil Rights era, held that the Sixth Amendment right to counsel was sufficiently "fundamental and essential to a fair trial" as to make it binding on the states through the Fourteenth Amendment.[7] In so holding, Justice Black wrote: "Not only [the earlier] precedents but also reason and reflection require us to recognize that in our adversary

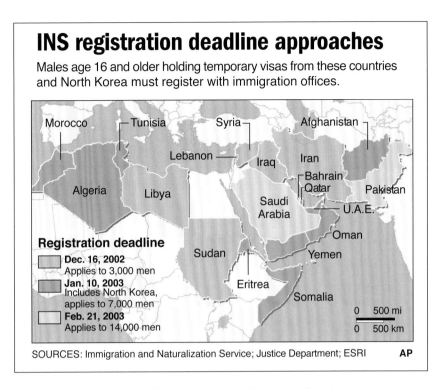

INS registration deadline approaches

Males age 16 and older holding temporary visas from these countries and North Korea must register with immigration offices.

Morocco — Tunisia — Syria — Afghanistan

Lebanon — Iraq   Iran

Bahrain
Qatar

Algeria   Libya   Pakistan

Saudi
Arabia   U.A.E.

Oman

Registration deadline

Dec. 16, 2002
Applies to 3,000 men

Jan. 10, 2003
Includes North Korea,
applies to 7,000 men

Feb. 21, 2003
Applies to 14,000 men

Sudan   Yemen

Eritrea

Somalia

0   500 mi
0   500 km

SOURCES: Immigration and Naturalization Service; Justice Department; ESRI   **AP**

New laws after September 11, 2001, required male immigrants age 16 and older who originated in certain countries (shown above) to register with U.S. immigration offices. The INS was replaced by the USCIS in 2003, but the regulations still stand.

system of criminal justice, any person haled into court, who is too poor to hire a lawyer, cannot be assured a fair trial unless counsel is provided for him."[8]

Though the cases have differed somewhat on the exact timing, the Sixth Amendment right to assistance of counsel attaches once the government has initiated charges against the accused. In *Kirby v. Illinois*, Justice Stewart wrote:

The initiation of judicial criminal proceedings is far from a mere formalism. It is the starting point of our whole system of adversary criminal justice. . . . It is then that a defendant finds himself faced with the prosecutorial forces of organized society, and immersed in the intricacies of substantive and procedural criminal law. It is this point, therefore, that marks the commencement of the "criminal prosecutions" to which alone the explicit guarantees of the Sixth Amendment are applicable.[9]

The right thus extends to investigation and preparation of a defense and, significantly, it also includes the defendant's right to communicate with an attorney. Open, two-way communication between attorney and client—free from government scrutiny—is required for the Sixth Amendment protection to be meaningful. Therefore, concludes Professor Cohn, a violation of the attorney-client privilege violates a defendant's right to effective assistance of counsel.[10]

This proposition is also reflected under treaty law—specifically, the International Covenant on Civil and Political Rights, ratified by the United States on June 8, 1992. Under this treaty, a criminal defendant is given the right to counsel and the right "to communicate with counsel." The right to counsel arises, as under U.S. common law, once a defendant has been criminally charged.[11] Defendants are guaranteed adequate time and facilities to prepare their defense, access to documents and evidence required for the defense, and that the defendant and attorney may communicate "in conditions giving full respect for the confidentiality of their communications." Arguably, then, the United States violates a treaty, which is binding under the supremacy clause of the Constitution, every time prison officials monitor communications between inmates and their attorneys.

Law enforcement officials have made it difficult for detainees to exercise their right to counsel.

Although the Department of Justice has not commented on the ability of September 11 investigation suspects to have counsel present during interrogations, it has insisted that their right to counsel for the purposes of immigration proceedings has been respected. In testimony before the Senate on December 7, 2001, Michael Chertoff, then–assistant attorney general (he became head of the Department of Homeland Security in 2005), said:

> Every one of [the detainees] has the right to counsel. Every person detained has the right to make phone calls to family and attorneys. Nobody is being held incommunicado….We don't hold people in secret, you know, cut off from lawyers, cut off from the public, cut off from their family and friends. They have the right to communicate with the outside world. We don't stop them from doing that.[12]

Fair Treatment

In July 2004, Majid al-Massari, a former University of Washington computer specialist and Saudi national whose exiled father is a vocal critic of their homeland's government, was targeted for a visa violation over a previous misdemeanor drug conviction. Immigration officials, however, focused on his alleged ties to terrorism. Al-Massari's worried coworkers did not know what happened until federal agents charged into their offices days later.

James Yee, a West Point graduate and third-generation Chinese American, was a decorated Army captain and one of the first Muslim chaplains in the service. In September 2003, while on his way home for a routine leave, Yee was detained and then held in shackles. His family would find out days later through cable news that he was being held on suspicion of espionage.

Although former Captain James Yee was released after 76 days of solitary confinement, al-Massari, 35, fought for two years in the hope of reversing an immigration judge's final decision in 2005 to deny him asylum. His supporters said he was in danger of torture and perhaps death if he returned to Saudi Arabia because of his well-publicized dissident opinions. He was deported in early 2007.

Source: "Friends Push for Fair treatment of Saudi Detainee," *Seattle Post-Intelligencer*, October 31, 2005; http://seattlepi.nwsource.com/local/246531_fast31.html.

Despite these claims, other parties, specifically a watchdog group called Human Rights Watch (HRW), stated that many post–September 11 detainees have not been able to exercise their right to counsel effectively.[13] For example, some detainees have not even been informed of their right to counsel.

Immigration detainees do not have the right to a free, court-appointed attorney under U.S. law, but they must be informed of their right to be represented by an attorney.[14] Many immigration detainees are unfamiliar with U.S. laws and do not know they are allowed to have an attorney present during any official questions. In a report conducted by HRW, 27 immigration detainees were interviewed. Only 10 said that they were informed of their right to an attorney.[15]

In one instance, the attorney for an Egyptian citizen told HRW that officials at what was then the Immigration and Naturalization Service (INS) refused to tell him where his client was detained for two weeks, during which time the client was transferred several times to different facilities.[16] The attorney said that it was only after he filed a petition with federal court that he was informed that his client was being held at the Passaic County Jail in New Jersey. The attorney also said that he called the INS daily for five days to find out when his client's deportation hearing might be held. On the fifth day, an official told him that the hearing had already taken place. Charged with improperly working while on a tourist visa, the client had waived the right to an attorney and plead guilty. The client was deported on November 30, 2001.[17]

While INS detainees long faced difficulties in terms of access to counsel, the aftermath of September 11 made conditions worse.[18] The INS's transfer policy was a common impediment to obtaining and keeping legal representation: The agency frequently moves detainees from one facility to another, with no thought given to where detainees' attorneys are based or where their families live. Furthermore, the INS did not give advance notice of transfers to detainees, families, or their lawyers. This resulted in the situation of attorneys unable at times to locate their clients. Furthermore, because of licensing limitations, attorneys sometimes were not able to continue to represent clients transferred to facilities in other states. After September 11, a new rule prohibited facilities from disclosing the identity of immigration detainees they hold; this made it even more difficult for lawyers to track down their clients.[19]

According to data from the Executive Office for Immigration Review, 80 percent of the immigration detainees that appeared before immigration courts in 2001 were not represented by counsel.[20] Many immigration detainees have very limited financial resources, which is perhaps their main obstacle in obtaining legal counsel. Post–September 11 detainees face even greater legal expenses because their cases involve unique complications, which require more expertise and time on part of the attorney.

A good example of the FBI's refusal to respect the right to counsel is that of Osama Awadallah, a lawful permanent resident of the United States and a citizen of Jordan. When an old phone number of Awadallah's was found in the car abandoned by Nawaf Al-Hazmi, one of the September 11 alleged hijackers, the FBI subsequently began an investigation of Awadallah.[21] On September 20, 2001, a team of eight FBI agents and local police officers went to Awadallah's apartment in San Diego. When Awadallah returned home early that afternoon, the agents told him they wanted to ask him a few questions at the FBI office. Awadallah asked if they could talk to him at his apartment, but they insisted that he be interviewed at their offices; they told him that they would drive him there. When Awadallah insisted he be allowed to go into his apartment to pray first, he was followed in by the agents, who patted him down and made him keep the bathroom door open while he urinated and washed before praying. When he was taken to the FBI office around 3:00 P.M., Awadallah repeatedly said that he did not want to miss a computer class he was to attend that evening. Despite this, the agents questioned Awadallah for about six hours and told him they believed he had information regarding the events of September 11. When he asked about getting to his class, the agents told Awadallah that he

INS agents process some of the 250 illegal Chinese immigrants who were dumped from a freight ship in San Francisco's harbor in 1993. Immigrants who are desperate to enter the United States may do so despite language barriers and other hardships, which in turn may make it difficult for them to receive fair treatment in their dealings with immigration officials.

would "have to stay" with them until the interview was finished. Although these circumstances indicate a custodial interrogation, during which he was entitled to an attorney, Awadallah was never informed of this right.

The interview ended at 11:00 P.M., and Awadallah agreed to take a lie detector test the following morning. The next morning, after he took the test, FBI agents said he had lied on some of the questions and accused him of being "one of the terrorists." Awadallah asked to call his lawyer, but the agents refused his request. They continued to question him, even though Awadallah repeated several times that he had to leave for Friday prayer. The agents told him he was going to miss Friday prayer and that they were going to fly him to New York. Awadallah again demanded to call a lawyer because it was his right, but the agents said, "[h]ere you don't have rights." The FBI subsequently secured a warrant for Awadallah's arrest as a material witness. He was later charged with perjury for lying to a grand jury. He spent 83 days in prison before being released on bail.[22]

In a subsequent court case, Awadallah claimed that he had been unlawfully seized by FBI agents. In their decision, the court pointed out that "a consensual encounter ripens into a seizure, whether an investigative detention or an arrest, when a reasonable person under all the circumstances would believe he was not free to walk away or otherwise ignore the police's presence."[23] Reviewing the facts, the court concluded that Awadallah was "clearly not 'free to ignore' the FBI" and had in fact been "seized." The seizure was illegitimate because the agents did not have probable cause or even reasonable suspicion to believe that Awadallah had committed a crime. Based on this and other findings of unlawful government conduct, the court dismissed the indictment against Awadallah. Although the question of Awadallah's right to an attorney was not raised in the case, the court's finding that he had been seized by the FBI when he was questioned implies that he should have been informed of his rights and given access to an attorney.

Attorney-client privilege must be preserved in immigration cases.

It is important to understand the purpose and the policy behind the long-standing attorney-client privilege to better grasp whether or not this privilege has been restricted or infringed upon. The attorney-client privilege is one of the oldest privileges based in common law.[24] Many scholars argue that the premise for the attorney-client privilege can also be found in the Sixth Amendment to the United States Constitution.[25] Due to its rich history, attorney-client privilege has been recognized as one of the most appreciated and respected privileges in American jurisprudence. In interpreting the privilege, however, the Supreme Court noted that it must be viewed "in light of reason and experience."[26] It will therefore adapt and change to reflect technological advancements and society's views in modern times.

The attorney-client privilege protects as confidential all information and communications shared between an attorney and a client during the process of obtaining and rendering legal advice, subject to a few exceptions. The purpose of the privilege is to promote full and frank communications between attorney and client, so that the client receives the best legal advice possible. The privilege is a necessary building block in ensuring that justice is served. Lawyers can only provide helpful and appropriate legal advice when their clients tell them the whole truth. Without the assurance of the attorney-client privilege, a client would never tell the entire story to his lawyer, which would make it impossible to provide proper and effective legal assistance. Ensuring the client that the attorney must keep certain information confidential allows the client to speak freely. In return, the client receives better legal advice, and administration of justice is served.

On June 20, 1997, the Bureau of Prisons finalized interim regulation, Section 28 CFR 501.3, authorizing special administrative measures, or SAMs, on a specialized group of inmates that presented a danger of disclosing information to third parties; such information could result in death or serious bodily injury to people on the outside.[27] That is, these inmates were thought to have information that, if passed on to someone outside of prison—perhaps via a lawyer—could lead to the injury or death of people outside of the jail. The rule provided that the attorney general, or the head of a federal law enforcement or intelligence agency, could make a written determination of whether specific inmates caused this particular type of threat. The inmates were able to seek review of any of the special administrative measures (SAMs) imposed by the regulation. Examples of these SAMs include housing in administrative detention or limiting certain privileges, such as visiting, correspondence, and use of the telephone.

Before the amendment to the Department of Justice Bureau of Prisons rule in 2001, attorney-client privilege protected all confidential communications between the attorney and the inmate that were made in order to obtain and deliver legal advice. Under the crime-fraud exception, if the government had a reasonable suspicion that communication between the attorney and the client was being used to plot a violent crime or terrorist activity, the law enforcement agency's only remedy was to go to court; a judge could determine if there was probable cause to disrupt those communications to prevent violent crime or terrorist activity. This was required even when the threat was life-endangering and imminent.

Much like drug kingpins and mobsters, members of al Qaeda had been known to use visits from their attorneys to relay information to the outside.[28] An "al-Qaeda terrorism manual [was] obtained overseas that urged members to take advantage of prison visits to communicate useful information to the outside."[29] This included prison visits with coconspirators or even the inmates' lawyers. Use of this tactic created a dangerous situation in which a terrorist attack could occur at any moment. In order to protect Americans from terrorists who used this strategy, the Department of Justice amended the Bureau of Prisons Regulation under the advisement of Attorney General John Ashcroft.

The amended rule provided that under certain circumstances, communications between the attorney and the inmate could be monitored when it was necessary to deter future acts of violence or terrorism.[30] The Bureau of Prisons regulation now gives more authority to the attorney general to pierce the attorney-client privilege under certain circumstances. If the attorney general has a reasonable suspicion that the lawyer-client communications are being used to facilitate acts of violence or terrorism, law enforcement officials can listen in on those conversations.

Civil libertarians have heavily criticized the procedure under the Bureau of Prisons regulation.[31] They assert that the attorney general has the sole authority to determine whether there is a "reasonable suspicion" that certain communications with attorneys are being used to facilitate violence or terrorist activity.[32] This standard is less than the probable cause standard set out in the Fourth Amendment to the United States Constitution.[33] The purpose of the probable cause standard is to protect the individual's privacy interests. Because the Bureau of Prisons regulation uses the reasonable suspicion standard, it is highly questioned and criticized as circumventing legislative authority and interfering with the fundamental right of privacy. The reasonable suspicion standard usually only applies to those situations where there is an imminent threat of harm to a civilian or officer, as in "stop and frisk" situations.[34] However, critics differentiate the intrusion on an inmate's conversations with an attorney from the "on the spot" action, which requires the lesser standard of reasonable suspicion. As a result, this regulation is viewed as a vehicle that could lead to a violation of the Fourth Amendment, stemming from its reasonable suspicion standard.

Also, the regulation was passed swiftly, as was the Patriot Act, and in the eyes of civil libertarians, this created a dangerous opportunity for the Department of Justice to use its powers destructively. The regulation was enacted unilaterally by the attorney general without the usual protections of notice and public comment afforded by the Federal Administrative Procedures Act.[35] It was posted in the Federal Register on October 31, 2001, only one day after it went into effect.

In order for the attorney general to determine whether or not to listen to the communications between an attorney and a client, he must first determine whether or not he has suspected that inmate of being involved in terrorism or acts of violence. In Section 802, the Patriot Act defines "acts of violence" and "domestic terrorism" in ways that make civil libertarians wary.[36] Prior to this new definition of terrorism, there were three other defined types of terrorism already set forth in federal law: international terrorism, terrorism transcending national borders, and federal terrorism. Now, a person can also be charged with domestic terrorism if:

> [W]ithin the U.S. they engage in activity that involves acts dangerous to human life that violate the laws of the United States or any State and appear to be intended: (i) to intimidate or coerce a civilian population; (ii) to influence the policy of a government by intimidation or coercion, or (iii) to affect the conduct of a government by mass destruction, assassination or kidnapping.[37]

Civil libertarians claim that this new definition is unnecessary, and it will subject everyday protestors to prosecution for terrorism. The General Accounting Office released a study in January 2003 that concluded that 75 percent of those convicted under the Patriot Act of "international terrorism" after September 11, 2001, were actually dealing in more common nonterrorist crimes.[38]

The American Bar Association and the National Association of Criminal Defense Lawyers also agree that allowing the monitoring of attorney-client communication violates the privilege, and that it is a serious infringement on the Sixth Amendment right to counsel.[39] The Sixth Amendment states, "[i]n all criminal prosecutions, the accused shall enjoy the right . . . to have the Assistance of Counsel for his defense."[40] The amendment recognizes the rights of the accused to speak confidentially with a lawyer. Under the confines of the new regulation, the accused may have a profound fear of being overheard, and he may not feel able to speak freely with his attorney. This is coupled with the fact that many detainees must already deal with the language barrier between themselves and their attorneys. It is also likely that they know little about the American legal system, including the role that their lawyer plays in the system. The American Bar Association and the National Association of Criminal Defense Lawyers have commented on the chilling effect the regulation will have on attorney-client communications.[41] They argue that the repercussions of the regulation will seriously restrict the effectiveness of counsel, thereby violating the Sixth Amendment of the Constitution.

Summary

Detainees not only have a constitutional right to access to an attorney, they also should enjoy the attorney-client privilege, which protects those conversations with counsel. Most people held in custody get to speak with an attorney without the threat of the government listening in. Immigrants also should be afforded those same safeguards in order that justice be served.

Immigrants Should Not Have Full Rights to Legal Counsel

The Bill of Rights, and in particular the Fifth Amendment's due process clause, guarantees certain protections to all "persons" regardless of their citizenship status.[1] For more than a century, however, the Supreme Court has narrowly interpreted constitutional protections in the immigration context, giving deference to federal discriminatory measures that would be impermissible if applied to citizens. In doing so, the Court has based its decisions in part on the federal sovereignty, national security, and foreign affairs powers implicitly or inherently stated in Article I of the Constitution.

Commonly referred to as the plenary power doctrine, federal immigration power is thought to be free from judicial review because it rests on the federal government's power to make rules that protect national sovereignty. Therefore, the federal government can discriminate against immigrants on the basis of national origin or similar factors, whereas this would be illegal if applied to citizens or by state governments. With the strength of plenary power, Congress has considerable leeway in setting the standards for naturalization of aliens and the power to regulate the behavior of aliens admitted into the country. Immigration officials may take race into account in making investigatory immigration stops, and the State Department and executive branch in general have great discretion in setting the terms for an alien's exclusion from the country.[2]

Immigrants do not have the right to a free attorney.

The Sixth Amendment does provide that every person accused of a crime is entitled to an attorney, and this right does extend to immigration hearings. What does not and should not extend to immigration hearings is the burden of providing an attorney at no cost to the immigrant. Free counsel should be provided only for U.S. citizens. The right to have an attorney appointed to an immigrant who cannot afford one has never, in jurisprudential history, been extended.

The theory behind appointing an attorney at no cost to criminal defendants is based on the potential for the loss of their liberty as protected by the Constitution.[3] Detainees held because of their potential involvement in terrorism should not be afforded court-appointed attorneys because the detainees have no standing in the United States. These immigrants are being held because they are connected with terrorism and therefore will never be admitted into the United States under any circumstances. To force American taxpayers to provide them with assistance of counsel would open the doors to providing counsel free of charge in all immigration hearings and potentially all administrative hearings.

Immigration hearings are administrative in nature. Although immigrants are permitted access to an attorney, the Supreme Court has never extended the right to have a court-appointed attorney at these hearings. The statute specifically states "at no cost to the Government" when it refers to appointed counsel. There are thousands of detained immigrants in custody every day. To supply each of them with a government-appointed attorney would cost the country millions of dollars, mostly to remove aliens who entered the United States illegally. The taxpayers should not bear that burden when the statute does not require it.

Due process is not limitless. Due process is satisfied by protecting the interests of those persons involved in removal proceedings by providing them access to an attorney. Due process does not, however, require that the government foot the bill for that attorney.

Privileged communications with an attorney.

The Patriot Act and Ashcroft's amendment to the Bureau of Prisons regulations were enacted to combat the immediate threat of terrorism. Civil libertarians often forget to mention the catalyst for enacting the amendments when they attack them as being unconstitutional. It must be remembered that, in times of war and when there are increasingly heavy threats of future terrorism, promoting national security is the most important goal on the government's agenda.[4] The Framers of the Constitution supported the notion that, in times of war and threatened national security, the government should have the power to deal with those threats.[5]

The United States is presently involved in the largest and most intense criminal investigation in the world. Effectively, the main objective must be to expand and enhance terrorism legislation to prevent any future terrorist attack. There are rational governmental goals behind the restrictions on inmates' attorney-client communications. In order to fully accomplish these goals, surveillance teams and law enforcement agencies need efficient tools to combat these threats before they occur. It is not enough to remedy terrorism after it occurs.

There is a reasonable balance between national security and civil liberties when utilizing the defense mechanisms set out in the Patriot Act and the Bureau of Prisons regulations.[6] Specifically, certain conversations and communications between terrorists and their attorneys, which serve as tools for terrorists to promote acts of violence and terrorism, should be monitored as part of these prevention procedures.

Civil libertarians who oppose the Patriot Act first argue that the procedures used by the Justice Department and the attorney general are extra tools that are not needed to combat terrorism and prevent imminent acts of violence. Those procedures, it is said, create the possibility that officials will misuse their authority. But the Patriot Act and subsequent legislation, such as the Bureau of Prisons regulation, have proven very effective and helpful in fighting terrorism. They have increased the investigator's ability to deal with terrorism activities, including weapons offenses, weapons of mass destruction, and terrorism financing. This legislation is necessary to enable law enforcement officials to "effectively monitor and track the enemy before their horrific plans come to fruition."[7]

Based on the statistics, it is evident that a more restrictive agenda, exemplified in the Patriot Act and the procedures followed by the Department of Justice, has been effective in catching those identified as dangerous suspects involved in terrorism. These procedures were necessary to identify and disrupt 150 terrorist cells since September 11, 2001.[8] Two-thirds of al Qaeda's known senior leadership has also been caught or killed, including the masterminds responsible for participation in the attacks of September 11, 2001. Other terrorist cells in major cities across the United States have been destroyed, and in the long-term, the Department of Justice is building a stronger network against terrorism. Although it is too early to calculate the efficiency of the amendment to the Bureau of Prisons regulation, it is the next logical step to prevent those captured from keeping contact and involvement with their collaborators who have not yet been caught.

Furthermore, civil libertarians urge citizens to believe that these procedures are tactics used against all American citizens convicted of ordinary crimes. In 2001, however, only 16 out of

158,000 individuals were even assigned to special administrative status, making them available for monitoring.[9] Additionally, these monitoring processes are similar to the processes used to determine if there is a crime-fraud exception in which a judge is given sole discretion to make the determination.[10]

Immigration Amendment to the Constitution

Many scholars have suggested that there will soon be an amendment to the U.S. Constitution to solidify immigrants' status with regard to the Bill of Rights. What is the process of amending the Constitution? There are essentially two ways spelled out in the Constitution detailing how it can be amended. One method has never been used.

The first method is for a bill to pass both halves of the legislature, by a two-thirds majority in each. Once the bill has passed both houses, it goes on to the states. This was the route taken by all current amendments. Because of some long outstanding amendments, such as the Twenty-seventh, Congress will normally put a time limit (typically seven years) for the bill to be approved as an amendment (for examples, see the Twenty-first and Twenty-second).

The second method prescribed is for a constitutional convention to be called by two-thirds of the legislatures of the states, and for that convention to propose one or more amendments. These amendments are then sent to the states to be approved by three-fourths of the legislatures or conventions. This route has never been taken, and there is discussion in political science circles about just how such a convention would be convened and what kind of changes it would bring.

Regardless of which of the two proposal routes is taken, an amendment must be approved by three-fourths of states. The amendment as passed may specify whether the bill must be passed by the state legislatures or by a state convention. Amendments are sent to the legislatures of the states by default. Only one amendment, the Twenty-first, specified a convention. In any case, passage by the legislature or convention is by simple majority.

It is interesting to note that at no point does the president have a role in the formal amendment process (though he would be free to make his opinion known). He cannot veto an amendment proposal, nor a ratification.

Although the attorney general is given authority to determine what communications can be monitored, the "privilege team" must still gain permission from an independent judge to give the monitored communications to the prosecution team. Effectively, there are sufficient safeguards in place to mimic a detached magistrate overlooking the procedure.

Even though the Patriot Act and the Bureau of Prisons regulation were enacted in the month immediately following the September 11 attacks, it was not unreasonable or inconceivable to rely on the national government to act properly with regard to security as soon as possible. Americans expect that their government, including Congress, will react to the needs of the American people. At that moment, the American people needed protection from terrorist threats and invasions within their land. Reflecting these needs, the Patriot Act was passed with overwhelming bipartisan support. At that time, it was also not certain how imminent further acts of violence and terrorism were. Therefore, it was only proper that the government act as quickly as it did. Finally, those opposing the Patriot Act and the regulation amendment concerning the attorney-client privilege claim that the constitutional guarantee of privacy is infringed. However, the American people have not agreed with this argument. Shortly after September 11, 2001, 82 percent of Americans did not feel that their civil liberties were infringed upon; in fact, they agreed with the Bush administration's procedures to deal with terrorist criminal detainees.[11] Polls taken in 2003 exhibited public support again, noting that Americans still did not feel pressure on their civil liberties.[12] The importance of this is grounded in the fact that the government, including the Department of Justice and Congress, is working for the American people. The polls show that the people feel they are being represented properly while retaining their privacy and freedoms.

Summary

The government, through its powers guaranteed by the Constitution, can choose not to extend to aliens rights that citizens enjoy. As long as the due process clause in the Constitution is satisfied, Congress can choose to limit aliens' rights as it sees fit, given its plenary power. National security also dictates that certain safeguards be put in place, like listening to communication between attorney and client, when it is believed a terrorist act is being planned.

Indefinite Detention of Immigrants Violates the Constitution

On October 31, 2001, Ibrahim Turkmen was ready to leave the United States. A Muslim imam and citizen of Turkey, he had come to the United States a year earlier on a six-month tourist visa, but had found work in the country at a gas station and for a construction company, and had overstayed his visa in order to send money back to his family in Turkey.[1] On October 18, 2001, FBI agents arrested Turkmen at his home, informally accused him of being associated with Osama bin Laden—a charge he denied and that was never formally advanced—and ordered him to immigration proceedings for overstaying his visa. Turkmen agreed to leave the country, and an immigration judge granted him "voluntary departure," a form of relief that allows aliens to leave the country without incurring the penalties associated with a final deportation order. Two days later, a friend purchased a plane ticket to Turkey for Turkmen and brought it to the Immigration and Naturalization Service office in Newark, New Jersey. In ordinary times, Turkmen would have been back in Turkey in a matter of days.

But these were not ordinary times, and the INS would not let Turkmen go. He remained in detention for another three and a half months, not because the INS faced any problems in effecting his removal, and not because the government had probable cause to believe that Turkmen had been involved in any criminal activity, but simply because the FBI had not yet cleared Turkmen in its investigation of the terrorist attacks of September 11. On February 25, 2002, when the FBI finally cleared Turkmen of any ties to terrorism or the events of September 11, the INS finally allowed him to leave.

Turkmen was not the only person detained unreasonably. Asif-ur-Rehman Saffi, a French citizen and native of Pakistan, was also detained in connection with the September 11 investigation and ordered deported on October 17, 2001. Instead, he remained in INS custody for four and a half months more and was actually deported only after the FBI had also cleared him. On February 18, 2002, the *New York Times* reported that, as of that date, 87 noncitizens were in the same situation: they had received voluntary departure or final deportation orders, but had been kept locked up and barred from leaving because the FBI was still investigating them.[2]

Had Turkmen or Saffi been U.S. citizens, there would have been no basis for their detention. They were never charged with any crimes and were not shown to pose any danger to the community or potential for flight risk. Moreover, once they were ready and willing to leave the country, there was not even any arguable immigration purpose for detaining them, as their custody was not necessary to effectuate their removal. They were held, in essence, "for investigation." Yet beyond the narrow confines of the brief stop-and-frisk authorized in *Terry v. Ohio*, the Constitution provides no justification for "investigative detention."[3] As the United States Supreme Court has recently stated, preventive detention is a narrowly carved exception to the general due process rule, which says that people may not be deprived of their liberty absent a criminal conviction.[4]

Due process should limit the government's ability to detain immigrants.

The detention of aliens for months beyond the time necessary to complete their removal is just one component of a wide-ranging preventive detention campaign undertaken by the Department of Justice after the attacks of September 11. In this campaign, the government has aggressively used immigration authority to implement a broad strategy of preventive detention where other civil or criminal law authority would not permit custody. By a conservative estimate, the government has arrested between 1,500 and 2,000 people since September 11 in connection with the investigation of the terrorist crimes committed that day.[5]

In November 2002, not a single person arrested in the preventive detention campaign had been charged with any involve-

The "Wilson 4"

In June 2002, four undocumented high school students drew the attention of immigration officials while attending an academic competition near Buffalo, New York. Three years later, "the Wilson 4" (named after the high school they attended), remain in limbo. The students were scheduled for deportation to Mexico. However, immigration Judge Richardson threw out the case, ruling that border agents engaged in unlawful racial profiling. The Justice Department has appealed the decision. The "Wilson 4" became undocumented aliens when their parents brought them to the United States as toddlers, a fate shared by approximately 65,000 other high school students each year. The pending DREAM Act legislation provides a glimmer of hope, giving undocumented students who have grown up in the United States and graduated from high school here a chance to apply for legalization.

Source: NPR, "The Nation," October 22, 2005.

ment in the September 11 attacks. (The only person so charged, Zaccarias Moussawi, was actually arrested before September 11.) Only four detained individuals have been charged with any terrorist-related crime.[6] The vast majority, like Turkmen and Saffi, have been cleared by the FBI of any involvement in the September 11 attacks or any terrorist activity of any kind. Thus, virtually all of the 1,500 to 2,000 people detained in the government's investigation of September 11 have turned out to be innocent of any involvement in terrorism.

The majority of the detainees have been held on immigration charges, again like Turkmen and Saffi. In some cases, the charges were highly technical. One man, Ali Maqtari, a lawful permanent resident alien, was held for a month on the charge that he had been out of lawful status for 10 days while adjusting his status from visitor to permanent resident. It is likely that the INS never deported anyone on such a charge; the purpose of his detention was not to enforce the immigration laws, but to detain him while the FBI interrogated and investigated him for a potential terrorism connection. When the FBI cleared him, he was released, and his charges were conditionally dropped pending a showing that his marriage was "genuine."[7]

Those held on immigration charges have been detained and tried entirely in secret. Their cases are not listed on any public docket, and the immigration judges presiding have been instructed to neither confirm nor deny that any particular case exists. Every aspect of the proceedings, no matter how routine, is closed to the public, to the press, and even to family members of the accused. After an immigration regulation issued in October 2001, the INS officials who prosecuted deportation cases could effectively override immigration judges who ruled that an alien should be released on bond while waiting for his deportation proceedings. The rule meant that when INS prosecutors filed to appeal such an order, the alien would be kept in custody without any requirement that the prosecutors show that their appeal was likely to succeed, or that

Detainees' Lawsuits

Between October and December 2001, several September 11 detainees with final orders of removal and voluntary departure orders filed lawsuits, or threatened to file lawsuits, to challenge their continued detention. The following are examples of cases in which detainees challenged their continued confinement.

Two September 11 detainees filed a lawsuit against the Department of Justice in the Northern District of Ohio on December 18, 2001, when the INS did not allow them to leave the country after they had received voluntary departure orders from an immigration judge. Two weeks prior to filing the petition for release, the detainees' attorney wrote the INS asking, among other things, "[u]nder what specific legal authority does the INS and/or the Department of Justice propose to prohibit these young men from returning home?" The INS did not respond to the attorney's questions. The attorney filed the December 18, 2001, habeas corpus petition asserting that it was unlawful for the United States to prohibit the detainees from leaving the country. The next day, the detainees received final clearances from the FBI and were permitted to leave the country.

A September 11 detainee who received a voluntary departure order from an immigration court had until November 23, 2001, to leave the country. That date passed with the INS refusing to release the detainee because the FBI had not issued a clearance letter; it had not received the CIA checks. Consequently, the INS's district director extended the time for the detainee's voluntary departure past November 23, 2001, to prevent the voluntary departure order from converting to a removal order (which would result in more restrictive consequences to the detainee).

The detainee's attorney filed a habeas corpus petition seeking his release on November 27, 2001. An e-mail from an INS attorney to an official at the INS noted that, while the INS attorney handling the case in the district had made the "eminently reasonable" assumption that the detainee "must be a serious criminal or terrorist," that assumption was not correct. The attorney explained that "the only reason [the detainee] remains on the list is for the CIA to run checks. It had been in that posture for at least two weeks." He wrote that "there is no evidence [the detainee] is a terrorist or is of interest to the FBI." In an earlier communication, the attorney had asked "how should the Service [INS] proceed. Should the Service continue to hold an individual for whom there is a final order, is on hunger strike, and for whom the FBI has no interest, in order for an administrative function to be completed, when that function is, for reasons unknown to me, taking in excess of two weeks?"

The acting director of the National Security Law Division forwarded the attorney's comments to the INS's General Counsel, and noted that this detainee's case was discussed regularly. Another INS attorney noted in an e-mail to a regional counsel that the alien's attorney had "threatened to go public and tell the Islamic community not to cooperate with the government ... because the only thing that will happen is that they would be locked up indefinitely. The timing of this is horrible, coming as it does in the middle of the Attorney General's effort to interview all those other folks." The alien was removed from the United States on December 4, 2001.

These examples indicate that the INS generally avoided addressing the substantive legal issues raised in the habeas corpus lawsuits by obtaining FBI clearance for an individual detainee who had filed a legal action before a formal response was needed on the merits. The INS first would argue that the detainees failed to exhaust all administrative remedies, thereby avoiding the primary legal question of whether the Department had legal authority to continue holding these detainees until the FBI could complete its clearance investigations. Other aliens in similar circumstances, who did not have attorneys or had attorneys who did not file habeas petitions, remained in custody.

Witnesses from the FBI, the INS, and the Criminal Division stated that the habeas cases were a top priority for the Justice Department, and that members of the Deputy Attorney General's office were aware of the issues in these cases, including the legal claims brought by the aliens challenging the INS's authority to detain them. Staff members for the Deputy Attorney General's office dispute this. For example, the senior counsel in the DAG's office told the Office of the Inspector General that she does not recall being aware of the details of the habeas petitions, nor does she recall any of the petitions raising the 90-day issue.

Source: U.S. Department of Justice Report on the September 11 Detainees, available at http://www.usdoj.gov/oig/special/0306/chapter6.htm#II.

there was a danger of irreparable harm if the alien were allowed to go free.

When the government is criticized for this use of immigration authority, its defenders often respond that those held on immigration charges are here unlawfully; as illegal aliens, they are subject to detention. Congress has recently imposed mandatory detention on various categories of aliens. In 1996, for example, Congress mandated detention of all aliens charged with having committed "aggravated felonies," a term in immigration law that sweeps far more broadly than it sounds, and encompasses even some misdemeanors. The same year, Congress mandated detention of at least some aliens who were already subject to final orders of deportation.

In the immigration setting, it is argued, preventive detention should be constitutionally permissible only when it aids in removal. The only legitimate purpose of immigration proceedings is to remove those aliens who do not have a legal basis for remaining in the United States. If the alien poses a flight risk, his detention may be necessary to ensure that he will be around if and when a final removal order is effective. If the alien poses a danger to the community, his detention may be necessary to protect the community while his legal status in the United States is resolved. But where an alien poses neither a danger nor a flight risk, his removal may be accomplished without detention, and detention therefore serves no legitimate government purpose. In such circumstances, detention is unconstitutional.

Due process places significant constraints on the government's power to detain individuals under its immigration authority. Immigration power cannot be used for punishment; that is, the government may not take a noncitizen's liberty without showing that the person poses a danger to the community or is a flight risk. Yet, immigration law in recent years has developed as if it were immune to these due process limitations. This is a relatively recent but widespread phenomenon.

The U.S. Supreme Court has already had one occasion to review it, and a second opportunity is currently pending. In

Zadvydas v. Davis (2001), the Court reaffirmed that, at least with respect to aliens living inside the United States, substantive due process applies with full force to immigration detention. Despite this, the government has found other ways to detain aliens.

The government has exploited the material witness rule.

Shortly after the terrorist attacks of September 11, 2001, Attorney General John Ashcroft directed federal law enforcement agencies to use "every available law enforcement tool" to arrest those who "participate in, or lend support to, terrorist activities."[8] Because it lacked reliable intelligence regarding potential terrorists in the United States, the Department of Justice adopted a policy of detaining any suspicious individual on a technical basis. Strict enforcement of minor immigration violations that had previously gone unenforced provided justification for the majority of the arrests.[9] But not every person whom agents deemed suspicious had violated an immigration regulation. In those cases, federal authorities needed another reason for legitimate detention. The solution was to arrest and imprison such suspicious people under the federal material witness statute, 18 U.S.C. § 3144, as witnesses to the grand juries convened in connection with the terrorism investigation.

On November 27, 2001, Attorney General John Ashcroft stated that as of that date, 248 people were being held on immigration charges, 104 people had been charged with federal criminal violations, and an unspecified number of other people were being held on material witness warrants.[10] A report by the Human Rights Watch indicates that, as of August 2002, the government held the vast majority of the detainees on immigration-related charges.[11] Human Rights Watch reported that most of the people held on immigration charges were from Pakistan, Egypt, and Turkey.[12] Human Rights Watch also reported that in the cases of people detained on material witness warrants, all of the detainees were held in federal prisons, many for several months, and often in conditions more restrictive than the conditions of the general criminal population.[13] Federal prison officials at the Manhattan Metropolitan Correctional Center in New York, where many of the detainees were held, reportedly designated the September 11 detainees as "high security inmates."[14] Prison officials also chose to keep the material witnesses segregated from the rest of the population and subjected them to "special precautions" including videotaping their movements.[15]

The requirements that a person neither be subjected to unreasonable seizures nor be deprived of liberty without due process of law are cornerstones of the American judicial system.[16] Since September 11, critics have accused the U.S. Department of Justice (DOJ) of seeking to circumvent these constitutional protections by using the material witness statute to arrest and hold persons thought to have information relevant to a grand jury investigation.[17] The material witness statute authorizes the arrest of material witnesses in "criminal proceedings."[18] The question arises: is a grand jury proceeding a "criminal proceeding" as that term is utilized in the material witness statute? The U.S. Supreme Court has made it clear that while the grand jury is necessary to the initiation of the criminal process, it is separate and apart from that proceeding. The purpose of a grand jury is to inquire into the existence of possible criminal conduct.[19] The grand jury is a "body of laymen, free from technical rules, acting in secret, pledged to indict no one because of prejudice and to free no one because of special favor."[20]

Indeed, many courts have characterized grand jury proceedings as civil, therefore the material witness rule does not apply to them. In *In Re Grand Jury Proceedings (Manges)*[21] the Ninth Circuit held that the 60-day notice requirement for civil appeals under the Federal Rules of Appellate Procedure 4(a) applied to contempt adjudications arising out of grand jury proceedings, implying that grand jury proceedings themselves are civil. The noncriminal nature of grand jury proceedings has also been recognized in the Third Circuit, which has held that a motion to quash a grand jury subpoena is a civil proceeding.[22] Similarly, in *United States v. Bonnell* a grand jury subpoena was treated as a civil action for purposes of certifying an appeal from an order refusing to stay its enforcement.[23]

In grand jury proceedings, there is no indictment until all the witnesses are examined and the grand jury has completed its work. No pleas are necessary because no one has been charged with a crime yet. Courts have held that civil procedures apply to grand jury proceedings and criminal proceedings require elements that grand jury proceedings lack. Therefore, grand jury proceedings are not plainly within the material witness statute's scope.

Investigating criminal behavior is a government interest, and this interest may justify a temporary seizure of a suspect or witness. For pretrial witnesses, the seizure is limited by the availability of depositions pursuant to Federal Rule of Criminal Procedure 15(a). That rule provides a "reasonable balance among the three competing interests that are at stake when a defendant is prosecuted: Society's interest in enforcing the law, a defendant's Sixth Amendment right to confront the witnesses against him, and a witness's liberty interest."[24] But the deposition procedure is unavailable to grand jury witnesses. The unavailability of a Rule 15 deposition "would eviscerate the limitation that Congress carefully placed upon the government's power to detain uncharged witnesses."[25]

As the *Awadallah* case illustrates, the intrusion upon Mr. Awadallah's liberty—and dignity—far exceeded any legitimate government interest. Mr. Awadallah was held under onerous, high-security prison conditions for 20 days before he was summoned to the grand jury.[26] Although he requested a deposition on his first appearance in court, that request was ignored. To him, any of the purported protections in the Material Witness Statute were, as Judge Schleindlin found, "meaningless," thereby denying him due process of law.[27]

September 11 detainees have been held without charge.

Individuals who are detained for a considerable length of time without charge fit into one of three categories: (1) war fighters from other countries detained on the battlefield, (2) U.S. citizens detained on the battlefield (the battlefield has been defined both as U.S. territory and foreign territory), and (3) noncitizens (unnaturalized aliens) who are living in the United States. These individuals are likely to be detained in one of three places: (1) a foreign country occupied by U.S. forces or in a foreign area controlled by U.S. forces, (2) Guantanamo Bay, Cuba, or (3) a standard legal detention facility in the United States. Guantanamo Bay is the site of a U.S naval base in Cuba. Located on the Southeast side of the island, it is the only naval base the United States has in a Communist country. The United States gained access to the base in 1903 under a leasing arrangement that makes cessation of the lease possible only if both sides agree or if the U.S. abandons the base. Although the U.S. leases the base, it concedes full sovereignty over the base to Cuba.

The U.S. agreement that Cuba retains full sovereignty over the base may have motivated the Bush administration to use Guantanamo to house all enemy combatants and others the United States wishes to detain indefinitely. The administration had hoped that the courts would agree that U.S. Courts have no authority over the base, though the courts have not accepted that and have intervened.

It is generally accepted that the president (acting as commander in chief) and the military have the authority to detain foreign enemy combatants without charge until the cessation of hostilities. Although prisoners of war must be treated in particular ways, they do not need to be charged with a crime unless held beyond the duration of hostilities. The authority of the president and the military to detain U.S. citizens on the battlefield (particularly on U.S. soil) without charge is somewhat more controversial. In the only known instance prior to this new September 11 era, a U.S. citizen who was accused of aiding and abetting the enemy was charged with a crime and tried in

(Opposite page) **After September 11, 2001, many immigrants were detained by the federal government for charges ranging from federal crimes to immigration violations.**

Detainees in the investigation

There are currently 603 people in federal custody, arrested as part of the terror investigation. A look at the types of charges filed to date:

Federal complaints and indictments   104

Fifty-five of the 104 people charges with federal crimes are currently being held in custody. Records of 93 cases have been unsealed by the Justice Department.

Immigration charges   548

All 548 people charged with violating immigration laws are being held in the custody of the Immigration and Naturalization Service. A breakdown of their countries of origin:

Europe

Albania, 2
Austria, 1
France, 2
Germany, 1
Spain, 3
United Kingdom, 2

Asia

Afghanistan, 4   Iran, 4   Kuwait, 3
Bangladesh, 6   Iraq, 3   Lebanon, 11
Cyprus, 1   Israel, 9   Nepal, 1
India, 20   Jordan, 17   Pakistan, 208
Indonesia, 1   Palestinian Territories, 1
Russia, 2
Saudi Arabia, 16
Syria, 9
Turkey, 47
Yemen, 38

North and South America

Brazil, 1
El Salvador, 1
Guyana, 8
Mexico, 1
Trinidad and Tobago, 2
Venezuela, 1

Africa

Egypt, 73   Mauritania, 4
Algeria, 5   Morocco, 15
Congo, 1   Senegal, 2
Congo Republic, 1   South Africa, 1
Eritrea, 1   Sudan, 1
Ivory Coast, 1   Tanzania, 2
Kenya, 2   Tunisia, 11
Libya, 1

Australia, 1

Immigration and federal charges combined   10

Ten people have been charged with both federal and immigration violations; they are among those listed above in each category.

State and local charges

An undisclosed number of people have been charged in state and local jurisdictions.

Material witnesses and local charges

An undisclosed number of people are detained as material witnesses, meaning they are believed to have information important to the investigation.

SOURCE: Justice Department   AP

a civilian court. The authority of the president and the attorney general to indefinitely detain unnaturalized aliens is even more, and arguably the most, controversial since it affects the greatest number of people. The authority for these indefinite detentions was created both before and after September 11 under legislation that will be discussed shortly.

Some of the authority that the attorney general claims for detaining without charge unnaturalized aliens not engaged in direct hostile action against U.S. forces is found in the Patriot Act. Under the Patriot Act, the attorney general has expansive powers to indefinitely detain noncitizens and individuals who are identified as contributing directly or indirectly to terrorist operations. As long as the attorney general has "reasonable grounds" to believe that person at issue is "described in" the antiterrorism provisions of the law, the individual is subject to indefinite detention.[28]

Nancy Chang explains that the authority to detain non-citizens springs from Section 411 of the Patriot Act that authorizes the attorney general to detain for as long as seven days noncitizens that he has "reasonable grounds to believe" are involved in terrorism without charging him or her with an immigration or criminal violation.[29] Although the seven-day window to charge seems reasonable, the government often claims that there are necessary circumstances that prevent a charge from being issued within that time period. The authority to detain noncitizens does not stem exclusively from the Patriot Act, however. Some authority also springs from changes made shortly after September 11. On September 17, 2001, well before the Patriot Act was passed, the Code of Federal Regulations (CFR) was amended to permit indefinite detention of aliens without arrest or bringing charge against them.[30]

The amendment to the CFR has gone a long way toward creating this fear. In times of "emergency or extraordinary circumstance," as the post-September 11 era has been called, immigration officials may detain individuals indefinitely, following a warrantless arrest, without bringing any charges against them. The amended rule provides no definition of emergency or extraordinary circumstance, nor any explanation of how long "an additional reasonable period" of detention may be. It is important to note that many individuals, particularly unnaturalized aliens, who are subject to indefinite detention have been charged with a crime—usually a minor immigration violation (most of those detained are immigrants). Chang explains that if a non-citizen is "certified" as a terrorist and charged with an immigration violation, he or she is "subject to mandatory detention without release on bond until either he is deported from the United States or the attorney general determines that he should no longer be certified as a terrorist."[31] Chang continues to explain that "Section 412 does not direct the Attorney General to notify the non-citizen of the evidence on which the certification is based, or to provide him with an opportunity to contest that evidence, either at an immigration judge hearing or through other administrative review procedure."[32]

The rationale for detention without charge is basically an argument in favor of preventive detention—detaining someone in order to prevent him or her from committing a crime. The government contends that if these individuals are released they could commit terrorist acts or support the commission of terrorist acts. In 2003, in *Denmore v. Kim,* the Supreme Court upheld a statute mandating preventative detention of foreign nationals during deportation proceedings, even if the person posed no risk of flight or danger to the community.

Unnaturalized immigrants—immigrants who do not yet have their citizenship but are in the United States—are usually detained under one of the previously discussed authorities. There are other categories of detained individuals—U.S. citizens detained at home and U.S. citizens detained abroad. The government claims that the authority to detain U.S. citizens as "enemy combatants" comes from two places. The first is the "Authorization to Use Military Force" (AUMF) against Afghanistan. The AUMF states that the president has the power to "use all necessary and appropriate force against those nations, organizations, or persons he determines planned, authorized, committed, or aided the terrorist attacks" or "harbored such organizations or persons, in order to prevent any future acts of international terrorism against the United States by such nations, organizations or persons." The second is its Plenary Power under article II of the Constitution. The government relied on both of these in the *Hamdi* case that will be discussed below, but the court only evaluated the AUMF argument, finding that the government had the authority to detain Hamdi under the AUMF.

The Supreme Court provided some hope of relief to those detained as enemy combatants. Yaser Esam Hamdi was accused of being an "enemy combatant" because he was captured in Afghanistan during "the conflict" and was "affiliated" with a Taliban unit. All the evidence the government relies on is a summary of testimony from Michael Mobbs, who interviewed Hamdi shortly after his capture in Afghanistan. Mobbs' synopsis is now known as the Mobbs Declaration. After Hamdi was captured, he was returned to the United States, where he was not permitted to meet with any attorneys. His father intervened as a Next Friend, and a public defender who was assigned to the case became actively involved. The attorney argued that since "the conflict" (the war on terror) had no definable endpoint and since the government never established what Hamdi's affiliation was, Hamdi could essentially be locked up for life and never able to challenge his designation as an enemy combatant.

Hamdi originally found a sympathetic ear in U.S. District Judge Robert Doumar (Norfolk, Virginia). Doumar was skeptical of the government's assertion that Hamdi was an enemy combatant and wanted to look at the evidence certifying him as such. The government challenged Doumar's request, however, arguing that it may need to disclose sensitive intelligence information in order prove that Hamdi was an enemy combatant. The government found a sympathetic ear in the U.S. District Court for the Fourth Circuit, which intervened, arguing that proper deference should be given to the military. But the appellate court chief judge, J.

Harvie Wilkinson, would not embrace the proposition that under no circumstances would judicial review of the "enemy combatant" designation be permitted, but that it could be permitted in only a very limited manner.

Detainee Case Study

One September 11 detainee was held at the Metropolitan Detention Center (MDC) in Brooklyn from October 16, 2001, until June 14, 2002. His wife said she experienced repeated problems while attempting to visit her husband. The woman, who took unpaid leave from work to travel from her home in New Jersey to the MDC, said that between October and December 2001 she was told by staff at the MDC that her husband was not incarcerated at the facility when, in fact, he was. When she eventually learned her husband was at the MDC, she visited him for the first time on December 19, 2001, after being granted a "special visit" by the unit manager at a date and time outside the normal visiting schedule. From January 31 to March 31, 2002, the woman said she was not permitted to visit her husband because he was being disciplined for failing to stand up for a 4:00 P.M. daily count.

The woman subsequently was permitted to visit her husband during the week of April 2, 2002. However, she was not permitted to visit her husband the week of May 1, 2002, because she arrived at the MDC on a day and at a time that MDC reception area staff told her was not the appropriate time to visit detainees held in the administrative maximum (ADMAX) Special Housing Unit (SHU). The woman told the Office of the Inspector General (OIG) that she assumed this was an appropriate time because it was the same day of the week and hour of her previous "special visit." When she contacted the ADMAX SHU unit manager about this particular visitation problem, he arranged for another "special visit" which took place on May 4, 2002. On May 9, 2002, the detainee's wife arrived at the MDC to visit her husband but MDC staff told her that all the visitation rooms were full. She was asked to wait until after the 4:00 P.M. inmate count for a possible visit at 4:30 p.m. At 4:30 P.M., the reception staff told her to go home and call the following day. On May 10, 2002, the detainee's wife said she was unsuccessful in contacting anyone at the MDC to arrange a visit with her husband.

Source: U.S. Department of Justice Report on the September 11 Detainees, available at http://www.usdoj.gov/oig/special/0306/chapter7.htm#VB.

In *Hamdi*, the majority of Supreme Court justices took issue with the appeals court decision and held that

> although Congress authorized the detention of combatants in the narrow circumstances alleged in this case, due process demands that a citizen held in the United States as an enemy combatant be given a meaningful opportunity to contest the factual basis for that detention before a neutral decision maker.

Justices O'Conner, Rehnquist, Kennedy, Breyer, Souter, and Ginsburg all agreed on this point, though Souter and Ginsburg did not even think the detention was authorized in the first place.

Most recently, in January of 2005, in *Clark v. Martinez*, the Supreme Court ruled 7 to 2 that the federal government cannot indefinitely imprison immigrants who cannot be deported even if they are in the country illegally. This decision also limited detention of immigrants to no longer than six months.

Civil liberties and human rights advocates applauded the ruling. "It adds to the growing list of Supreme Court rulings affirming the rights of noncitizens and overturning the Bush administration's overreaching claims," said Lucas Guttentag, director of the ACLU Immigrants' Rights Project, whose organization filed written arguments in court. "It points to the crucial role of judicial oversight over executive decisions."[33]

Summary

Indefinite detention is a violation of the Due Process clause of the U.S. Constitution. All persons held in connection with the terrorist bombings of September 11, 2001 are entitled to due process and therefore should be charged or released, not held indefinitely until the "war on terror" concludes.

Indefinite Detention of Immigrants Does Not Raise a Constitutional Concern

In times of perceived threats to national security, individual rights are often at risk. The security of the state may trump the rights and freedoms that individuals otherwise expect. How seriously individual rights are disregarded or undermined depends on how extensive they were to begin with. In constitutional democracies, where the rule of law is prized, where the concept of rights is deeply ingrained in the national culture, and where the protection of rights is considered one of the government's highest priorities, the dilemma is particularly crucial. It may not be literally true that, to quote an old Roman maxim, *Inter arma silent leges* ("During war, law is silent") but there can be little doubt that in such times, both rights and the rule of law are changed.

Article I, Section 8, Clause 4 of the Constitution grants Congress the power to establish a "uniform Rule of Naturalization." From this has developed the "plenary power doctrine," which holds that Congress has complete authority over immigration matters. The Supreme Court has said that "over no conceivable subject" is federal power greater than it is over immigration.[1] Because of this the Court has said elsewhere, "In the exercise of its broad power over naturalization and immigration, Congress regularly makes rules [affecting immigrants] that would be unacceptable if applied to citizens."[2]

Detainees are granted appropriate due process.

In the case of *Hamdi vs. Rumsfeld*, Justice Sandra Day O'Connor wrote that even though an alleged enemy combatant "must

FROM THE BENCH

Rasul v. Bush

The U.S. Supreme Court in *Rasul v. Bush* held that foreign nationals imprisoned without charge at the Guantanamo Bay interrogation camps were entitled to bring legal action challenging their captivity in U.S. federal civilian courts.

Justice John Paul Stephens' majority opinion was joined by Justices Sandra Day O'Conner, David Souter, Ruth Bader-Ginsburg, and Stephen Breyer. Justice Anthony Kennedy joined in the decision but disagreed sufficiently with the majority's analysis to issue a separate concurring opinion. Justice Antonin Scalia authored a dissenting opinion, joined by Chief Justice William Rehnquist and Justice Clarence Thomas.

The decision addressed the question of "whether United States courts lacked jurisdiction to consider challenges to the legality of the detention of foreign nationals captured abroad in connection with hostilities and incarcerated at the Guantanamo Bay Naval Base, Cuba."

Consistent with the historic purpose of the writ, this Court has recognized the federal courts' power to review applications for habeas relief in a wide variety of cases involving executive detention, in wartime as well as in times of peace. The Court has, for example, entertained the habeas petitions of an American citizen who plotted an attack on military installations during the Civil War, *Ex parte Milligan,* 4 Wall. 2, 18 L.Ed. 281 (1866), and of admitted enemy aliens convicted of war crimes during a declared war and held in the United States, *Ex parte Quirin,* 317 U.S. 1, 63 S.Ct. 2, 87 L.Ed. 3 (1942), and its insular possessions, *In re Yamashita,* 327 U.S. 1, 66 S.Ct. 340, 90 L.Ed. 499 (1946).

receive notice of the factual basis for his classification, and a fair opportunity to rebut the Government's factual assertions before a neutral decision maker," the degree of due process would be commensurate with "the nature of the case."[3] Because of the ongoing war on terror, "the exigencies of the circumstances may demand that, aside from these core elements, enemy combatant proceedings may be tailored to alleviate their uncommon potential to burden the Executive at a time of ongoing military conflict."[4]

Since the government might find it difficult to present a strong factual case justifying the detention of an enemy combatant, the

---

In *Rasul v. Bush*, Justice Stevens wrote, "The question now before us is whether the habeas statute confers a right to judicial review of the legality of executive detention of aliens in a territory over which the United States exercises plenary and exclusive jurisdiction, but not 'ultimate sovereignty.'"

The Court reversed the U.S. District Court for the District of Columbia and the Court of Appeals for the D.C. Circuit, which had held that the Supreme Court's 1950 decision in *Johnson v. Eisentrager* barred Guantanamo detainees from bringing actions challenging their detentions in U.S. courts because they were foreign nationals outside U.S. sovereign territory. Justice Stevens continued:

> Application of the habeas statute to persons detained at the base is consistent with the historical reach of the writ of habeas corpus. At common law, courts exercised habeas jurisdiction over the claims of aliens detained within sovereign territory of the realm, as well as the claims of persons detained in the so-called "exempt jurisdictions," where ordinary writs did not run, and all other dominions under the sovereign's control....
>
> In the end, the answer to the question presented is clear. Petitioners contend that they are being held in federal custody in violation of the laws of the United States. No party questions the District Court's jurisdiction over petitioners' custodians....We therefore hold that §2241 confers on the District Court jurisdiction to hear petitioners' habeas corpus challenges to the legality of their detention at the Guantanamo Bay Naval Base.

Source: *Rasul v. Bush* 542 U.S. 466, 474-475 (U.S. 2004)

Court's flexible due process standard "would not be offended by a presumption in favor of the government's evidence, so long as that presumption remained a rebuttable one and fair opportunity for rebuttal [by the detainee] were provided."[5] In a civilian criminal proceeding, the defendant is presumed innocent until he is proven guilty beyond a reasonable doubt. In a civil proceeding, the side that produces a "preponderance of the evidence," showing that its story is more likely than not to be true, wins.[6] But in an enemy combatant hearing as outlined by O'Connor, the government is granted a powerful presumption in favor of its case.[7]

Immigrants subject to a discriminatory deportation law would retain procedural rights with respect to its implementation.[8] In addition, Supreme Court jurisprudence has afforded more procedural protections to certain immigrants based on their connections to the United States. Immigrants with significant legal ties to the United States and immigrants actually within the borders of the United States, for instance, are entitled to greater protections.[9]

On the other end of the spectrum, however, are detainees who are held on suspicions of criminal activity or because they may pose a threat to national security. Detainees suspected of being involved in terrorism are being held in Guantanamo Bay, Cuba. The United States leases this land from Cuba for a military base, with the understanding that it remains Cuba's jurisdiction. The issue at hand is whether terror-war detainees held at Guantanamo Bay are entitled to contest their detention under habeas corpus.

Due process, which is guaranteed by the Fifth and Fourteenth Amendments, is a flexible concept. The process that is due depends upon the specific set of circumstances in a particular case. For example, a criminal defendant facing murder charges is entitled to a high level of procedural rights. In contrast, a public school student undergoing disciplinary proceedings is subject to a lesser standard.

In June 2004, the U.S. Supreme Court decided in *Rasul v. Bush* that the detainees at Guantanamo are entitled to the protections of the U.S. judicial processs even though they are not American citizens and are physically imprisoned outside the United States. The majority opinion in that case, written by Justice John Paul Stevens, said that the facility at Guantanamo Bay is under the "complete jurisdiction and control" of the United States, according to the 1903 lease from Cuba.[10] Because of this, the argument goes, the detainees are considered to be in U.S. sovereign territory and should not be denied habeas privileges.

There is "legitimate difference of opinion as to what exactly the Supreme Court said" in their decision on the case.[11] Some scholars interpreted the ruling to mean that the Guantanamo detainees have a right to be heard but have no legal basis for a case; while others interpreted the ruling more broadly, believing that detainees have the same rights as American citizens to contest their detention in U.S. courts. The interpretation that best fits with precedent is to limit the decision to apply only to habeas corpus appeals (and denying other sorts of suits), in order to determine if

FROM THE BENCH

Hamdan v. Rumsfeld

Hamdan was an enemy combatant incarcerated in a U.S. military detention facility and charged with various terrorism-related offenses. He was designated for trial before a military commission and he petitioned for habeas relief.

> Hamdan claims that AR 190-8 entitles him to have a 'competent tribunal' determine his status. But we believe the military commission is such a tribunal. The regulations specify that such a 'competent tribunal' shall be composed of three commissioned officers, one of whom must be field-grade. AR 190-8 § 1.6(c). A field-grade officer is an officer above the rank of captain and below the rank of brigadier general—a major, a lieutenant colonel, or a colonel. The President's order requires military commissions to be composed of between three and seven commissioned officers. 32 C.F.R. § 9.4(a)(2), (3). The commission before which Hamdan is to be tried consists of three colonels. We therefore see no reason why Hamdan could not assert his claim to prisoner of war status before the military commission at the time of his trial and thereby receive the judgment of a 'competent tribunal' within the meaning of Army Regulation 190-8.

Source: *Hamdan v. Rumsfeld* 415 F.3d 33, 43 (C.A.D.C. 2005).

the detainee is being held properly. This would allow the government to secure the safety of the United States as well as provide some limited protection to the detainees.

In response, Congress passed the 2005 Detainee Treatment Act (DTA), which governed treatment and interrogation of detainees at Guantanamo, but also was applied to prohibit aliens held at Guantanamo from suing in federal court for any reason.

The DTA was challenged in *Hamdan v. Rumsfeld*, in which the Supreme Court ruled that the act only referred to future cases—pending cases, those that had already been filed, could proceed. By ruling in this way, the Supreme Court decided the case on statutory grounds, thus avoiding having to confront the broader constitutional issue of whether habeas corpus extended to the Guantanamo detainees at all. Before long, however, another court would take on the challenge.

Habeas Corpus

Habeas corpus is Latin for "you have the body." Prisoners often seek release by filing a petition for a writ of habeas corpus. A writ of habeas corpus is a judicial mandate to a prison official ordering that an inmate be brought to the court so it can be determined whether or not that person is imprisoned lawfully and whether or not he should be released from custody. A habeas corpus petition is a petition filed with a court by a person who objects to his own or another's detention or imprisonment. The petition must show that the court ordering the detention or imprisonment made a legal or factual error. Habeas corpus petitions are usually filed by persons serving prison sentences. In family law, a parent who has been denied custody of his child by a trial court may file a habeas corpus petition. Also, a party may file a habeas corpus petition if a judge declares her in contempt of court and jails or threatens to jail her.

In *Brown v. Vasquez*, 952 F.2d 1164, 1166 (9th Cir. 1991), the court observed that the Supreme Court has "recognized the fact that '[t]he writ of habeas corpus is the fundamental instrument for safeguarding individual freedom against arbitrary and lawless state action.' *Harris v. Nelson*, 394 U.S. 286, 290-91 (1969)." Therefore, the writ must be "administered with the initiative and flexibility essential to insure that miscarriages of justice within its reach are surfaced and corrected."*

In 2006, the Military Commissions Act (MCA) was signed into law in part in response to the Supreme Court's decision in *Hamdan.* The act's stated purpose was "to facilitate bringing to justice terrorists and other unlawful enemy combatants through full and fair trials by military commissions, and for other purposes." The act was challenged in the U.S. Court of Appeals for the District of Columbia Circuit in the case of *Boumediene v. Bush.* In this case, Guantanamo detainees contested their imprisonment, claiming a right to habeas corpus. Their petitions for review were pending when the MCA was signed into law, and their defense contended that the MCA, like the DTA, only applied to future cases, not those that were already in motion. The District Court ruled that in fact the MCA applied to all cases, present and future, and thus the detainees had no standing in court to challenge their detention. Boumediene and his codefendants appealed the case, and in June

The writ of habeas corpus serves as an important check on the manner in which state courts pay respect to federal constitutional rights. The writ is "the fundamental instrument for safeguarding individual freedom against arbitrary and lawless state action."** Because the habeas process delays the finality of a criminal case, however, the Supreme Court in recent years has attempted to police the writ to ensure that the costs of the process do not exceed its manifest benefits. In *McCleskey v. Zant*, the Court raised barriers against successive and abusive petitions. The Court raised these barriers based on significant concerns about delay, cost, prejudice to the prosecution, frustration of the sovereign power of the States, and the "heavy burden" federal collateral litigation places on "scarce federal judicial resources," a burden that "threatens the capacity of the system to resolve primary disputes."***

The Court observed that "[t]he writ of habeas corpus is one of the centerpieces of our liberties. `But the writ has potentialities for evil as well as for good. Abuse of the writ may undermine the orderly administration of justice and therefore weaken the forces of authority that are essential for civilization.'"

* Harris, 394 U.S. at 291.
** *Harris v. Nelson*, 394 U.S. 286, 290-91 (1969).
*** *McCleskey v. Zant*, 499 U.S. 467 (1991).

2007, the U.S. Supreme Court granted a writ of certiorari, indicating that it would hear their appeal in October 2007.

As the District Court indicated in *Boumediene*, never has a U.S. court stated that an alien outside U.S. sovereign territory has a right to the protections of the U.S. Constitution, including habeas corpus. Because the Guantanamo detainees are held outside of the United States, they have no right to challenge their detention through the U.S. courts, and their indefinite detention does not raise a constitutional concern.

All of this has bearing on immigrants to the United States because they, too, can be considered aliens until they establish themselves as permanent residents. If the U.S. government determines that an immigrant is a threat, he or she could be detained at a location that, like Guantanamo, is outside of American sovereign territory, meaning that the immigrant would have no recourse to challenge such detention. The courts have ruled, however, that under certain circumstances, the government does retain the right to detain non-U.S. citizens without granting them habeas relief.

Immigrants may be detained for other reasons, too. One such situation involves the use of the material witness rule. When a witness's testimony is both relevant to the issue at hand and required to resolve the matter, they are known as a material witness. In order to resolve court cases, people who are material witnesses can be ordered to appear in court, and may even be detained if they are determined to be a flight risk. This material witness rule has been used, sometimes controversially, to detain some immigrants who have been subject to deportation proceedings.

The material witness rule has been used appropriately.

The Second Circuit's decision in *United States v. Awadallah*[12] and the Ninth Circuit's 1971 decision in *Bacon v. United States*,[13] both federal appellate decisions, address whether a grand jury proceeding is a criminal proceeding in the material witness context. Both courts held that grand jury proceedings fall under the material witness statute's scope. Both courts also recognized, however, that other appellate courts have specifically held that grand juries are not "criminal proceedings."

In *Bacon,* the Ninth Circuit court reasoned that Congress must have viewed criminal procedures and proceedings to include grand jury proceedings because Rule 2 of the Federal Rules of Criminal Procedure states that the federal rules are "intended to provide for the just determination of every criminal proceeding." Since the federal rules include both Rule 6, governing grand juries, and Rule 17, governing subpoenas, it can be inferred that these are considered criminal proceedings. But that reasoning, as the district court found in *Awadallah,* is false:

> Rule 2 does not define the phrase "criminal proceeding" as it is used throughout the Federal Rules of Criminal Procedure; nor does it help determine whether a grand jury is (or is not) a proceeding that necessarily comes before the initiation of a criminal proceeding as used in [former] Rule 46 ... Rule 17 may apply to grand juries, but it does not mention "criminal proceedings". Rather, it states: "A subpoena shall be issued by the clerk under the seal of the court. It shall state the name of the court and the title, if any of the proceeding and shall command each person to whom it is directed to attend and give testimony at the time and place specified therein." [14]

September 11 detainees do not qualify for immigrant or POW status.

The U.S. Department of Defense asserts that this is proper. According to the DOD, there is no requirement in the law of armed conflict that a detaining power charge enemy combatants with crimes, or give them lawyers or access to the courts in order to challenge their detention. In prior wars, nations have generally not done so. The Third Geneva Convention of 1949 accords prisoner of war (POW) status only to enemy forces who follow certain rules: wear uniforms; do not deliberately target civilians; and otherwise fight in accordance with the laws and customs of war. POW status guarantees the prisoner certain protections.

Al Qaeda and the Taliban militia fighters do not quality for POW status, however. As groups, they systematically and deliberately have attacked innocent civilians and they do not wear clothing that distinguishes them from civilians. Additionally, al Qaeda is not a party to the Geneva Convention and has no right under international law to wage war. As a result, the detainees from the groups at Guantanamo Bay need not be accorded the protections due to POWs.

Summary

Detention of enemy combatants in wartime is not an act of punishment. It is a matter of national security and military necessity. Detention prevents enemy combatants from continuing to fight against the United States and its partners in the war on terror. Releasing enemy combatants before the end of the hostilities and allowing them to rejoin the fight would only prolong the conflict and endanger coalition forces and innocent civilians.

There Is a Right of Access to Deportation Hearings in the Wake of 9/11

The Constitution is often interpreted as granting Congress absolute exercise of authority over immigration matters, leaving little room for judicial review. With the passing of the Immigration and Nationality Act in 1994, however, Congress delegated much of its power over immigration to the executive branch. This act granted the attorney general the power of "administration and enforcement" of "all . . . laws relating to the immigration and naturalization of aliens."[1] Based on this authority, then–Attorney General John Ashcroft enacted a regulation that governs public access to deportation hearings. On September 21, 2001, at the direction of Ashcroft, Chief Immigration Judge Michael Creppy issued a directive instructing all U.S. immigration judges to close all "special interest" deportation hearings to the public (including the media), and to friends and family members of the alien detainees. The Creppy Directive cited heightened security measures as the reason for the mandatory blanket closure on deportation hearings. Those who oppose the closure of deportation hearings say that there is a right of access to such hearings and that the blanket closure is unconstitutional.

There is a clear history of public access.

Even in the earliest days of the common law system, trials were considered to be open affairs. Jurors were members of the community of the accused and were responsible for bringing the accused before the judge and presenting the facts at the trial, thus being an integral part of the proceedings rather than simply observers. The jury has been described as "the lamp which shows that freedom lives"[2] and "the bulwark of our liberties."[3] Open courts are an almost inevitable consequence of our system of courts and the use of juries. Although much has changed in the legal system since those early days, one constant is that the general public has almost always been present at criminal trials.

The main argument for open trials is that they prevent judicial abuse by allowing the public to serve as a check upon the judicial process.[4] However convenient closed trials may appear at first, it should be remembered that delays and little inconveniences in the judicial process are the price that all free nations must pay for their liberty in more substantial matters. There are some legitimate reasons courts may close their proceedings to the public, including national security interests, but most immigration proceedings do not fit in this category.

Historically, newspaper reporters were given the same rights of access to observe judicial proceedings as the rest of the public. Reporters were allowed to report the court events in newspapers. These reports increased public awareness of the judicial process and the law, in addition to providing information about current events in general. This long-standing right of access originated in English common law, and the public's right of access to trials is considered fundamental to the legal system in the United States. The First Amendment of the Constitution indicates that Congress shall make no laws abridging the freedom of the press, and the

Sixth Amendment guarantees that in all criminal prosecutions, the accused shall enjoy the right to a public trial.

The *Richmond Newspaper* case established a right of access.

The Supreme Court established a First Amendment right of access to criminal proceedings in *Richmond Newspapers, Inc. v. Virginia.*[117] *Richmond Newspapers* involved a lower court's order to forbid news reporters from attending a criminal trial. Based on the common-law practice of holding hearings in front of the community, and the Bill of Right's concept of freedom of assembly, the Supreme Court held that criminal trials are places traditionally open to the public, and thereby the federal court cannot summarily close its courtroom doors. To this day, the Supreme Court has not explicitly applied this ruling to civil trials. However, federal courts have recognized that a trial is a public event and, as such, the press and the public have a presumptive right of access to civil and criminal proceedings.

Deportation hearings—or removal hearings, as they are now called—are highly adversarial in nature and look very much like a civil or criminal trial. Proceedings begin with the issuance of a document called a notice to appear. The respondent has the right to an attorney, although it is at his or her own expense. An immigration judge presides over the hearing, and "shall administer oaths, receive evidence, and interrogate, examine and cross-examine the alien and any witnesses."[5] INS chief counsel plays a prosecutorial role, and exercises broad "prosecutorial discretion." The respondent has the right "to examine the evidence against the [respondent,] to present evidence, . . . and to cross-examine witnesses."[6] Chief counsel has the right to cross-examine the respondent and present his or her own witnesses. The case in many ways resembles a criminal trial, albeit without a jury, and a respondent who has been ordered removed is subject to detention. The Federal Rules of Evidence, while not directly applicable, have influenced rulings on admissibility of evidence and objections to particular questions. In short, removal hearings "closely parallel[] the judicial model of decision-making."[7]

The *Richmond Newspapers* test applies to administrative proceedings.

Aside from criminal and civil courts, administrative panels also apply the *Richmond Newspapers* test in determining whether the press has a right of access. Courts reviewing administrative decisions also have found support for the presumption of public access to all or portions of administrative proceedings.

Allowing public access to administrative proceedings has also been examined in the immigration context. In *Pechter v. Lyons*,[8] a district court decided that an immigration judge abused his discretion in excluding the public from a deportation hearing. The court in *Pechter* reiterated that

> public policy [demands] that judicial proceedings, especially those in which the life or liberty of an individual is at stake [i.e., being deported from the United States], should be subject to public scrutiny, not only for the protection of the individual . . . but also to protect the public from lax prosecution.[9]

Although no other court examined the closure of removal proceedings since the decision in *Pechter* was announced, USCIS regulations provide for openness in immigration proceedings except for certain exceptions. For instance, immigration judges are instructed to limit or close removal hearings to protect the identity of witnesses, shield information about an abused alien spouse, or conduct a secret proceeding to receive classified or sealed documents.[10]

The Creppy Directive has enabled the violation of immigrants' rights with the inappropriate closure of hearings.

The Creppy Directive, in effect, gave immigration judges the authority to unilaterally label a case as special interest and close the hearing. Once a judge labels a case as such, it shuts the deportation-hearing doors, not only to the press and public, but also to the deportee's family. Any and all information about these hearings, including whether a case is even on the docket or scheduled for a hearing, is also concealed.

In *Detroit Free Press, et al., v. Ashcroft*, the immigration judge labeled a case "special interest," and, without notice to the defendant or his attorney, closed the hearing to the press and the public. The *Detroit Free Press* and other newspapers filed complaints seeking a declaratory judgment, arguing that the Creppy Directive violated their First Amendment right of access to the defendant's deportation proceeding. The Sixth Circuit Court found that the First Amendment does grant access to deportation hearings, so it granted the judgment and struck down the Creppy Directive because the policy was not "narrowly tailored," and was both underinclusive and overinclusive.

A few months later, in *North Jersey Media Group, Inc. v. Ashcroft*, the Third Circuit considered the same issue. Finding no First Amendment right of access to deportation, the court upheld the government's blanket closure of all "special interest" deportation hearings. Although both courts used the *Richmond Newspapers* "experience and logic" test (discussed below) in determining the public's First Amendment right to attend deportation hearings, they reached different conclusions. Those who oppose the closure of deportation hearings argue that the Sixth Circuit came to the correct conclusion.

Applying *Richmond Newspapers* shows that there is a right of access to deportation hearings.

In deciding whether the First Amendment affords the press and public a right of access to deportation hearings, the Sixth Circuit Court used a two-prong analysis, initially mentioned by Justice Brennan in *Richmond Newspapers*, and later formalized in *Press-Enterprise Company v. Superior Court of California for Riverside County*.[11] To recognize a First Amendment right of access to a hearing, the court must analyze both prongs of the "experience and logic" test of *Richmond Newspapers*. The "experience" prong considers whether the hearing has traditionally or historically afforded accessibility to the press and general public.[12] Even if the

North Jersey Media Group, Inc. v. Ashcroft

From November 2001 to February 2002, reporters for the *New Jersey Law Journal* and *Herald News* ("the Newspapers") were repeatedly denied docket information for and access to deportation proceedings in Newark's Immigration Court. On March 6, 2002, the Newspapers filed a federal court challenge to the Creppy Directive, asserting that its mandated policy of closing every "special interest" case precluded the case-by-case treatment the First Amendment requires. They argued not only that individualized inquiries are proper and practical, but also that because the directive permits special interest detainees themselves to disseminate information concerning their proceedings, its veil of secrecy is ineffective at best. North Jersey Media Group, Inc. v. Ashcroft 308 F.3d 198, 203 -204 (C.A.3 2002).

Whatever the outer bounds of *Richmond Newspapers* might be, they do not envelop us here. Deportation proceedings' history of openness is quite limited, and their presumption of openness quite weak. They plainly do not present the type of "unbroken, uncontradicted history" that *Richmond Newspapers* and its progeny require to establish a First Amendment right of access. We do not decide that there is no right to attend administrative proceedings, or even that there is no right to attend any immigration proceeding. Our judgment is confined to the extremely narrow class of deportation cases that are determined by the Attorney General to present significant national security concerns. In recognition his experience (and our lack of experience) in this field, we will defer to his judgment. We note that although there may be no judicial remedy for these closures, there is, as always, the powerful check of political accountability on Executive discretion.

The importance of this case has not escaped us. As we approached it, we were acutely aware that the countervailing positions of the parties go to the heart of our institutions, our national values, and the republic itself. Commenting upon the great national dilemma in which this case ineluctably embroils us—the eternal struggle between liberty and security—a number of newspapers have editorialized favorably upon Judge Keith's eloquent language in the *Detroit Free Press* case: "Democracies die behind closed doors,"…"When government begins closing doors, it selectively controls information rightfully belonging to the people. Selective information is misinformation."

Others have been less impressed. Michael Kelly has written in the Washington Post: *"Democracies die behind closed doors."* So they do, sometimes. But far more democracies have succumbed to open assaults of one sort or another—invasions from without, military coups and totalitarian revolutions from within—than from the usurpation-by-in-camera-incrementalism that Judge Keith fears.

Democracy in America does at this moment face a serious threat. But it is not the threat the judge has in mind, at least not directly. It is true that last September's unprecedented mass-slaughter of American citizens on American soil inevitably forced the government to take security measures that infringed on some rights and privileges. But these do not in themselves represent any real threat to democracy. A real threat could arise, however, should the government fail in its mission to prevent another September 11. If that happens, the public will demand, and will get, immense restrictions on liberties.

Although Mr. Kelly ultimately sided with openness on a case-by-case basis, we find his quoted statements powerful. They certainly seem appropriate to the decision to close the deportation hearings of those who may have been affiliated with the persons responsible for the events of September 11th, all of the known perpetrators of which were aliens. And they are consonant with the reality that the persons most directly affected by the Creppy Directive are the media, not the aliens who may be deported. As always, these aliens are given a heavy measure of due process—the right to appeal the decision of the Immigration Judge (following the closed hearing) to the Board of Immigration Appeals (BIA) and the right to petition for review of the BIA decision to the Regional Court of Appeals. *See also INS v. St. Cyr,* 533 U.S. 289, 300, 121 S.Ct. 2271, 150 L.Ed.2d 347 (2001) (noting that because the Constitution "provides the Writ of Habeas Corpus shall not be suspended, ... some judicial intervention in deportation cases is unquestionably required by the Constitution").

Because we find that open deportation hearings do not pass the two-part *Richmond Newspapers* test, we hold that the press and public possess no First Amendment right of access. In the absence of such a right, we need not reach the subsequent questions whether the Creppy Directive's closures would pass a strict scrutiny analysis and whether the District Court's "national in scope" injunction was too broad.

Source: *North Jersey Media Group, Inc. v. Ashcroft* 308 F.3d 198, 220 -221 (3d Cir. 2002), cert denied, 538 U.S. 1056 (2003).

court finds a tradition of openness to the public, it must still look to the "logic" test by finding a "significant positive role" in affording access to the public.

In deportation hearings, the noncitizen has the ability to defend himself and seek appropriate remedies. He is also afforded a number of fundamental rights that ensure fairness in these proceedings. For example, he has the right to ask for habeas corpus relief, a right to counsel, the right to be present at his own hearing, the right to examine the evidence used against him and present evidence on his own behalf, and the right to cross-examine witnesses.[13] Thus, deportation proceedings are very similar to judicial proceedings.

Because of the similarities between deportation and judicial proceedings, and because of the tradition of open judicial proceedings, the public should have a First Amendment right of access to deportation hearings. In ascertaining the significance of public access to deportation hearings, it is crucial to consider "whether access . . . is important in terms of that very process."[14] The beneficial effects of a First Amendment right of access may be so overwhelming and undeniable that a brief historical tradition alone may suffice to justify that access.

Although some exceptions have been permitted, deportation hearings have traditionally been open to the public. Congress has, from time to time, enacted statutes closing exclusion hearings, yet none of these statutes require closure of deportation hearings. In fact, deportation hearings have been presumptively open as a result of INS regulations promulgated since 1965. In *Detroit Free Press*, the Sixth Circuit Court noted that Congress has revised the Immigration and Nationality Act at least 53 times since then, and has never indicated that its intent was anything other than keeping deportation hearings open to the public.[15] Since Congress enacted statutes that explicitly close exclusion hearings, it could have just as easily enacted laws closing deportation hearings; however, Congress did not set forth such statutes. Even if one views Congress' silence as ambiguous, the Supreme Court has stated that "any lingering ambiguities in deportation statutes" should be interpreted "in favor of the alien."[16]

Open hearings keep the public informed, but they also advance fairness to the deportees themselves. After all, the Supreme Court has indicated that noncitizens are bestowed with all constitutional rights, including "due process" of law, once present in the United States. One important element of due process includes a fair hearing, and "[c]ourts have found that an open hearing is fundamental to guarantee a fair hearing."[17]

An important positive role of an open deportation hearing is to ensure that the government does its job properly, without mistakes. It is better for an immigrant to be improperly admitted than for a legal citizen to be improperly expelled. Naturally, it can be beneficial to the government to hold its meetings behind closed doors because it can avoid "criticism and proceed informally and less carefully," and thus, not worry about its prejudicial remarks being dragged into the headlines.[18] But, since deportees have no right to counsel at the government's expense, the press and public may be their only hope in ensuring them due process of law.

Summary

Centralizing immigration power in the hands of the government by closing deportation hearings to the public threatens the First Amendment right of access to hearings and jeopardizes due process of law. The government should not alter its adherence to the long-respected immigration procedures and protection of First Amendment rights in the name of national security. Adhering to these traditions would assure every American that, notwithstanding war or peace, the government functions consistently while respecting the fundamental liberties guaranteed by the U.S. Constitution.

National Security Requires That Immigration Proceedings Be Closed

In the wake of the attacks of September 11, 2001, lawmakers throughout the country sought to enact new policies to protect the citizens of the United States and prevent further attacks. In the course of investigating the attacks, officials determined that there were a number of immigrants to the United States who might have ties to the attackers or other terrorist groups. When it came time to hold hearings about the legal status of these suspicious individuals, officials found reason to worry about information being leaked to terrorist organizations via the public deportation hearings. On September 21, 2001, Chief Immigration Judge Michael Creppy, on the order of Attorney General John Ashcroft, closed all "special interest" deportation hearings to the public, where *special interest* was defined as "those in which the Federal Bureau of Investigation has a continuing interest because they relate to the government's terrorist investigations."

In February 2002, immigrants Ahmed Raza and Malek Zeidan were called to their deportation hearings in Newark, New Jersey. The two men's cases were declared of special interest and their trials were promptly closed, as per the Creppy Directive. In *North Jersey Media Group v. Ashcroft*, the North Jersey Media Group and the *New Jersey Law Journal* filed suit challenging that the closure violated their First Amendment right of access to the hearings. The trial judge agreed with the media's position and ruled that there was a presumptive right of access to deportation hearings and prohibiting enforcement of the Creppy Directive. The government appealed, and the U.S. Court of Appeals for the Third Circuit over-turned the lower court's decision, stating that the attorney general had the right to close the hearings for national security reasons. The case hinged on the media's claim of a right to access, but does the First Amendment really include this right?

The First Amendment guarantees that

> Congress shall make no law respecting an establishment of reli-
> gion, or prohibiting the free exercise thereof; or abridging the
> freedom of speech, or of the press…

This freedom of the press has commonly been read to govern the press' ability to publish information; i.e., the government may not punish the press for information that it disseminates (as long as it is not libelous), nor may the government exercise prior restraint—restraint of speech in advance of publication. In *Near v. Minnesota*, 283 U.S. 697 (1931), the Court struck down a Minne-sota state law that permitted public officials to seek an injunction to stop publication of any "malicious, scandalous and defamatory newspaper, magazine, or other periodical." In the majority opinion, Chief Justice Charles Evans Hughes called the law "the essence of censorship" and declared it unconstitutional. He further ruled that the government must prove "that publication must inevitably, directly, and immediately cause the occurrence of an event kindred to imperiling the safety" of individuals or national interest in order to justify a restraint prior to publication.

Though these press freedoms are well established, there is one that is still being questioned and shaped. If the government cannot prevent the press from printing information that the press already has, does this mean that the government must also provide access to all information? In other words, does the media have a right of access to information?

There may be a right of access, but the government may limit it.

There are several recognized categories in which the government does not have to provide information to the press. The most common reason for this is in matters of national security. After the Vietnam War, for example, the government began restricting journalists' access to battlefields. Previously, journalists had reported from alongside troops engaged in combat. As modern warfare has become more complex, though, the U.S. government has seen fit to place restrictions on this kind of access.

During the first Persian Gulf War, the U.S. Department of Defense (DOD) imposed a new set of press guidelines governing the functioning of press pools, the conduct of journalists, and standards of review for material prior to publication. In *The Nation Magazine, et al., v. United States Department of Defense*, the plaintiffs claimed that the pooling regulations unconstitutionally restricted the media's right of access and infringed on their newsgathering privileges.

The district judge for the case, Leonard B. Sand, wrote, "this case presents a novel question since the right of the American public to be informed about the functioning of the government and the need to limit information availability for reasons of national security both have a secure place in this country's constitutional history." Sand noted that the Supreme Court had observed in *First National Bank of Boston v. Bellotti* (1978), that "the First Amendment goes beyond protection of the press…to prohibit government from limiting the stock of information from which members of the public may draw." In addition, he cited *Branzburg v. Hayes*, 408 U.S. 665 (1972), in which the Court wrote "without protection for seeking out the news, freedom of the press could be eviscerated." Finally, Sand wrote,

> If the reasoning of these recent access cases [including *First National Bank, New York Times, Richmond Newspapers,* etc.] were followed in a military context, there is support for the proposition that the press has at least some minimal right of access to view and report about major events that effect the functioning of the government, including, for example, an overt combat operation…but this conclusion is far from certain.[1]

Sand determined that the plaintiffs had not presented a viable alternative to the DOD's system. Throughout the case, the plaintiffs maintained that the only solution was full, unrestricted access to military combat operations; they demanded that "the Court… hold, as a matter of constitutional law, that DOD follow only those guidelines used during the Vietnam War." In response to this request, Sand wrote "there is little similarity between the Vietnam War and Desert Storm. The traditional battlefield of the two World Wars and of Vietnam may be a phenomenon of the past."[2]

Given the precedent for the government's limiting media access to information, it seems that the government may limit access to government forums other than battlefields, especially where national security is implicated.

The right of media access to deportation hearings is limited.

The case of *Press-Enterprise v. Superior Court*, 478 U.S. at 1, codified what came to be known as the Richmond Newspapers "experience and logic" test. The experience prong was defined as "whether the place and process have historically been open to the press and general public." The logic prong was to determine "whether public access plays a significant positive role in the functioning of the particular process in question."

As mentioned previously, both the Sixth and Third Circuit Courts used to the *Richmond Newspapers* test to decide whether or not the Creppy Directive is unconstitutional. Their differing decisions, despite using the same test, hinged on their different evaluations of *Richmond*'s experience and logic prongs.

Although the Sixth Circuit found that the experience prong was fulfilled, the Third Circuit saw it a different way: "We ultimately do not believe that deportation hearings boast a tradition of openness sufficient to satisfy Richmond Newspapers,"[3] because in the 100-plus years of formal deportation hearings, they have not all been uniformly accessible. For example, many have been held in places where the public is not generally allowed access, such as private homes and in prisons.

The courts also differed in their evaluations of the logic prong, which asks whether statute at issue "plays a significant positive role" in the process. The Sixth Circuit looked exclusively at the role of access in terms of how it benefits the immigrant facing deportation, concluding that public access was an important way of ensuring that deportation hearings are fair. On the other hand, the Third Circuit looked at the potential negative effects of open hearings, for, in their words, "to gauge accurately whether a role is positive, the calculus must perforce take into account of the flip side—the extent to which openness impairs the public good."[4] The Third Circuit determined that the threats to national security posed by open hearings did not satisfy the logic prong.

> Since the primary national policy must be self-preservation, it seems elementary that, to the extent open deportation hearings might impair national security, that security is implicated in the logic test. When it is factored in, given due consideration to the attorney general's statements of the threat, we do not believe that the Richmond Newspapers logic prong test favors the media either.[5]

Information from deportation hearings may compromise national security.

In support of closing deportation hearings to the public, the government argues that preventing disclosure of information from

these cases is necessary for the following reasons: (1) Public iden-
tification of detainees could subject them to intimidation or harm;
(2) the identities of detainees' may prevent their cooperation with
the government; (3) the release of the detainees' names may reveal
the status of the government's investigation; (4) the release of the
detainees' identities could allow terrorist organizations to interfere
with the investigation by providing false evidence; and, (5) detainees who are later found to have no connection to terrorism may
be stigmatized.[6] The government further contended that "[b]its
and pieces of information that may appear innocuous in isolation" may be used by terrorists to create a "bigger picture" of the
government's terror investigation.[7] The government indicated that
this type of gathering of information is "akin to the construction
of a mosaic," where one isolated piece of information is not important until "pieced together with other pieces of information."[8]

In view of the government's compelling interest and all of its
concern, the Creppy Directive and its "blanket closure" of deportation hearings are necessary. The Department of Justice also created
interim rules, authorizing immigration judges to order detainees
and their attorneys from disclosing information. The interim rules
explicitly restrain deportees from communicating information for
an "indefinite period of time."[9] The Creppy Directive applies not
only to the "small segment of particularly dangerous information,"
but to all information in order to provide safety and security to the
nation. Courts may construe the protective orders to terminate at
the end of the deportation hearings, at which time nothing would
prevent the deportee from divulging all important information,
avoiding the constitutional issue raised by civil rights groups.

Trials should be closed if there are national security concerns.

In *North Jersey Media Group, Inc. v. Ashcroft*, the Third Circuit
emphasized the national security context and a tradition of deference to the government in such cases: "To the extent that the Attorney General's national security concerns seem credible, we will not
lightly second-guess them."[10] In a footnote, the court clarified,

The Creppy Directive

The following is excerpted from the memo included with the Creppy Directive.

Instructions for cases requiring additional security

Immigration Courts are beginning to receive cases for which the Department of Justice is requiring special arrangements....

  The following procedures are being followed for these cases:

1. Because some of these cases may ultimately involve classified evidence, the cases are to be assigned only to judges who currently hold at least secret clearance.

2. You should make certain that INS (or whoever provides your courtroom security) is informed of the hearing and the need to provide additional courtroom security.

3. Each of these cases is to be heard separately from all other cases on the docket. The courtroom must be closed for these cases—no visitors, no family, and no press.

4. The Record of Proceeding is not to be released to anyone except an attorney or representative who has an EOIR-28 on file for the case....

5. This restriction on information includes confirming or denying whether such a case is on the docket or scheduled for hearing. Any press requests must be referred to the Public Affairs Office....

6. The ANSIR record for the case is to be coded to ensure that information about the case is not provided on the 1-800 number and the case is not listed on the court calendars posted outside the courtrooms.

  ...

8. Finally, you should instruct all courtroom personnel, including both court employees and contract interpreters, that they are not to discuss the cases with anyone.

> We do not defer to the Executive on the basis of its plenary power over immigration…. The issue at stake in the Newspapers' suit is not the Attorney General's power to expel aliens, but rather his power to exclude reporters from those proceedings…. We defer only to the executive insofar as it is expert in matters of national security, not constitutional liberties.[11]

The Third Circuit gave considerable deference to the government's assertion that if a terrorist cell learned one of its members had been detained it might destroy evidence, modify its methods of entering the country or even accelerate plans for an attack.[12] "It seems elementary that, to the extent open deportation hearings might impair national security, that security is implicated in the logic test."[13] The court also rejected arguments that the hearings could be closed on a case-by-case basis, saying that the immigration judges did not have the expertise to overrule the attorney general on whether disclosure of a case would be harmful. "We are quite hesitant," the court said, "to conduct a judicial inquiry into the credibility of these security concerns, as national security is an area where courts have traditionally extended great deference to executive expertise."[14]

In *North Jersey Media Group*, the plaintiffs argued that a deportation hearing should be closed only if the government could convince a judge of the need for secrecy. The Third Circuit, however, sided with the government's contention that a case-by-case adjudication would reveal sensitive information and the only way to protect national security is by enforcing the Creppy Directive. They were convinced that sophisticated terrorists could piece together information suggesting a member of the group had been taken into custody. Additionally, a detainee, once deported, is free to divulge to the press any information learned during the proceedings. With the closure of such proceedings, the government attempted to protect information that seems "innocuous in isolation, but when pieced together with other bits and pieces … creat[es] a bigger picture" of the "mosaic intelligence."[15] In times of war, it is necessary to take precautions such as this.

Relying on the government's concept of "mosaic intelligence" to justify closed deportation hearings to the public sets the stage for future use of this argument in all immigration matters. Based on this precedent, the government can expand and extend national security concerns to encompass a large number of judicial matters that may ultimately result in more proceedings being conducted behind closed doors. Today, terrorism and national security are the issue, and protecting the public and national interests is the government's main priority.

When deportation hearings are conducted in secret, an innocent person who has lived and worked hard in this country for years would not be deprived of due process of law. The immigrant would still enjoy the constitutional safeguards of due process and access to an attorney. Closing hearings are a safeguard to prevent information from leaking to potential terrorist organizations.

Summary

National security dictates that certain immigration proceedings be closed to the public. In times of war, safeguards must be taken to protect national security and the public; part of this is the prevention of leaks to terrorist cells. Civil rights are important safeguards that protect the people from government infringement. Whether or not all of these rights are extended to noncitizens is an important question to raise. Noncitizens, whether they are legal or illegal aliens, could pose a threat to national security if they have ties to anti-American organizations. But this also true about citizens. The courts will have to decide whether it is just to deny non-citizens basic constitutional rights and other rights afforded to citizens.

The Future of Immigrants' Rights

Many experts believe that the discussions over how immigrants are treated in the wake of September 11, 2001, will continue for many years to come. Balancing national security interests with constitutional guarantees prove to be difficult for lawmakers and attorneys alike. Immigrants' rights will undoubtedly be in flux until the Supreme Court definitively steps in and dictates what rights and liberties immigrants enjoy when faced with national security concerns. Until then, debate will continue.

The great disagreement among lower courts in analyzing the substantive and procedural due process implications of mandatory immigration detention is in large part due to the absence of Supreme Court consideration of the due process rights of aliens. The 1990s saw an upsurge of challenges to mandatory detention provisions on due-process grounds. Many of the courts considering these challenges proceeded with a lack of relevant Supreme Court insight until the Supreme Court decided *Zadvydas v. Davis* in July 2001. Although the analysis and dicta in *Zadvydas* contribute greatly to this issue, its departure from precedent and the several questions it leaves open do not necessarily provide a decisive conclusion to the issue.

The Court's holding in *Zadvydas* certainly leads to the conclusion that detention of aliens during removal or deportation proceedings implicates a fundamental liberty interest. Despite the Court's willingness to apply a higher standard of scrutiny in an immigration context, the *Zadvydas* decision, together with an established line of immigration cases, indicates that detention of criminal and suspected terrorist aliens does not necessarily violate due process rights. Detention may be a permissible deprivation of an alien's liberty interest when it meets three conditions: it must be limited in time; narrowed to those that are particularly dangerous or pose flight risks; and limited by procedural safeguards. These safeguards should ensure the safety of citizens and other lawful aliens and ensure the efficacy of immigration laws in carrying out the immigration policy entrusted to Congress by the Constitution.

In the historical balance between Congress' plenary power over immigration and the due process rights of aliens, the courts, following by the holding in *Zadvydas*, began to prioritize due process concerns. The terrorist attacks of September 11, 2001, however, created a changing political climate that has shifted the balance. In response to the charges that the Immigration

(Opposite page) **The map illustrates the distribution of immigrants across the United States. In 2005, 12.1 percent of the U.S. population was born in another country, the highest percentage since 1920. With even legal immigration continuing to boom, discussions of immigrants' rights are likely to continue for years to come.**

Legal immigration continues to boom

About 12.1 percent of the current U.S. population was born in another country, the highest percentage since 1920. The total foreign-born population hit 35.2 million people in 2005.

Number of foreign-born immigrants per county, 2000

- 0 - 500
- 501 - 1,000
- 1,001 - 2,000
- 2,001 - 5,000
- 5,001 and more

Hispanic and Latino population per county, 2000

- 0 - 1,000
- 1,001 - 5,000
- 5,001 - 10,000
- 10,001 - 50,000
- 50,001 and more

SOURCE: U.S. Census Bureau   AP

and Naturalization Service failed to detect and remove terrorist aliens present in the United States, Congress and the executive branch have sought to strengthen immigration policy and law as tools to aid in the investigation and deterrence of terrorist attacks. The courts are likely to carefully reconsider the context of this legislation with great deference to Congress' political power over immigration.

The three branches of government must tread carefully on the new ground created by the tension between the political climate following the attacks of September 11 and the duty to respect the due process rights of an increasingly large number of immigrants in the United States. Congress must exercise its constitutional powers carefully to prevent overstepping its constitutional limits and remedy any such mishaps. Indeed, bills to amend the constitutional problems with the mandatory detention provisions have been repeatedly introduced in Congress. Most recently, the Restoration of Fairness in Immigration Act of 2002 was introduced in the House with the intention of amending mandatory detention provisions.

The executive branch must make sure to respect due process rights in its implementation of immigration law and any new duties delegated by Congress. The judicial branch must be sure to protect the due process rights of aliens while deferring to Congress and the executive branch in the political power over immigration granted by the Constitution. As a tool to protect the public and ensure the efficacy of immigration proceedings, mandatory detention is likely to survive only in limited situations, for limited durations, with sufficient procedural safeguards, and only of carefully defined individuals, such as terrorists or criminal aliens that indicate flight risks or imminent threats.

Introduction: Civil Liberties for Immigrants

1 Anser Mahmood's story is taken from http://www.refuseandresist.org/detentions/art.php?aid=970.

2 *Detroit Free Press v. Ashcroft*, No. 02-1437 (6th Cir. Aug. 26, 2002).

3 Indeed, only those amendments dealing with voting rights speak of the rights of citizens.

4 See, e.g., *Zadvydas v. Davis*, 533 U.S. 678, 679 (2001) ("[T]he Due Process Clause applies to all persons within the United States, including aliens, whether their presence is lawful, unlawful, temporary, or permanent."); *Yick Wo v. Hopkins*, 118 U.S. 356, 369 (1886) (stating that the Equal Protection Clause is "universal in [its] application, to all persons within the territorial jurisdiction, without regard to any differences of... nationality....").

5 See, e.g., *Zadvydas*, 533 U.S. at 693-94.

6 *Mathews v. Diaz*, 426 U.S. 67, 80 (1976).

7 The Uniting and Strengthening America by Providing Appropriate Tools Required to Intercept and Obstruct Terrorism Act of 2001, Pub. L. No. 107- 56, 115 Stat. 272 (2001). Available online [pdf]. URL: http://frwebgate.access.gpo.gov/cgi-bin/getdoc.cgi?dbname=107_cong_public_laws&docid=f:publ056.107.pdf.

8 See http://www.cis.org/articles/2001/back1501.html for an explanation of the Patriot Act Provisions.

9 Stephen Young, "Military Commissions: A Quick Guide to Available Resources," LLRX.com. Available online. URL: http://www.llrx.com/features/military.htm.

10 Council on Foreign Relations, "Terrorism Q&A: Military tribunals." Available online. URL: http://www.cnn.com/SPECIALS/2002/cfr/stories/tribunals/index.html.

Point: The Right to an Attorney is Being Ignored for Immigrants

1 Marjorie Cohn, "The Legal Profession: Looking Backward: The Evisceration of the Attorney-Client Privilege in the Wake of September 11, 2001," 71 Fordham L. Rev. 1233, 1234 (2003).

2 Max Radin, "The Privilege of Confidential Communication Between Lawyer and Client," 16 Cal. L. Rev. 487, 488 (1927-28).

3 Cohn, "The Legal Profession."

4 *Hunt v. Blackburn*, 128 U.S. 464, 470 (1888).

5 Ibid.

6 *Upjohn Co. v. United States*, 449 U.S. 383, 389 (1981).

7 *Gideon v. Wainwright*, 372 U.S. 335, 342, 344-45 (1963).

8 Ibid.

9 *Kirby v. Illinois*, 406 U.S. 682, 689-71 (1972).

10 Cohn, "The Legal Profession."

11 Sarah Joseph et al., *The International Covenant on Civil and Political Rights: Cases, Materials and Commentary*. 2nd ed. New York: Oxford University Press, 2004.

12 Testimony of Michael Chertoff, assistant attorney general of the Criminal Division, before the Senate Judiciary Committee at its hearing on "DOJ Oversight: Preserving Freedoms While Defending Against Terrorism," November 28, 2001.

13 Human Rights Watch, "Denial of Access to Counsel." Available online. URL: http://www.hrw.org/reports/2002/us911/USA0802-03.htm.

14 "Initiation of Removal Proceedings," 8 USC 1229 (a)(E).

15 Human Rights Watch, "Denial of Access to Counsel."

16 Ibid.

17 Human Rights Watch telephone interview with Martin Stolar, Ahmed Adbou El-Khier's attorney, New York, March 28, 2002. Available online. URL: http://www.hrw.org/reports/2005/us0605/12.htm#_ftnref260

18 Human Rights Watch, "Locked Away: Immigration detainees in jails in the United States," A Human Rights Watch Report, vol. 10, no. 1(G), September 1998.

19 8 CFR Parts 236 and 241, INS No. 2203-02.

20 The INS has refused to disclose how many of the thousand-plus "special interest" cases were unrepresented. Forced by a court order, the Department of Justice declared on June 13, 2002, that only 18 of the 74 "special interest" cases in

custody at the time did not have counsel (about 25 percent).

21 The phone number was that of a residence where Awadallah had lived briefly two years earlier. The FBI investigations subsequently established that Awadallah had no connections with or knowledge about the September 11 attacks or terrorist activities, but that he had met Al-Hazmi and another alleged hijacker at work and at the local mosque two years earlier when they lived in San Diego, California.

22 Second Opinion and Order, *United States of America v. Osama Awadallah*, 202 F. Supp. 2d 55 (S.D.N.Y. 2002).

23 Ibid., p. 38.

24 See *Upjohn Co. v. United States*, 449 U.S. 383, 389 (1981) (describing attorney-client privilege as oldest of confidential communications known in common law).

25 See U.S. Const. amend. VI (listing rights of accused in criminal prosecutions); see also *Noggle v. Marshall*, 706 F.2d 1408, 1413 (6th Cir. 1983) (stating that District Court has interpreted Sixth Amendment to include broad attorney-client privilege).

26 Fed. R. Evid. 501.

27 *United States v. Reid*, 369 F.3d 619, 621 (1st Cir. 2004) (explaining that SAM's could also be authorized if there was danger of "substantial damage to property that would entail the risk of death or serious bodily injury to persons" occurring)

28 Adam Cohen, "Rough Justice: The Attorney General has Powerful New Tools to Fight Terrorism. Has He Gone Too Far?", *Time*, Dec. 10, 2001, p. 30.

29 Ibid.

30 Rules and Regulations, Bureau of Prisons, U.S. Dep't of Justice, 28 C.F.R. § § 500, 501.3(d)(2)(i) (2002) (stating that inmate-attorney communications may be monitored to prevent future acts of terrorism).

31 Teri Dobbins, *Protecting the Unpopular from the Unreasonable: Warrantless Monitoring of Attorney Client Communications in Federal Prisons*, 53 Cath. U. L. Rev. 295, 301-02 (2004).

32 Mary Ellen Tsekos, Legislative Focus: Patriot Act, 9 Hum. Rts. Br. 35, 35 (2001) (stating that "Attorney General Ashcroft originally requested that law enforcement officials be able to detain individuals indefinitely without formal charges").

33 U.S. Const. amend. IV (setting forth probable cause standard for searches and seizures).

34 Gabriel M. Helmer, "Note, Strip Search and the Felony Detainee: A Case for Reasonable Suspicion," 81 B.U. L. Rev. 239, 288 (2001).

35 John W. Whitehead & Steven H. Aden, Forfeiting "'Enduring Freedom' for 'Homeland Security': A Constitutional Analysis of the USA Patriot Act and the Justice Department's Anti--Terrorism Initiatives," 51 Am. U. L. Rev. 1081, 1116 (2002).

36 Charles I. Lugosi, "Rule of Law or Rule by Law," 30 Am. J. Crim. L. 225, 273 (2003).

37 "How the USA-Patriot Act Would Convert Dissent into Broadly Defined 'Terrorism," ACLU Archives (Oct. 23, 2001) Available online. URL: http://archive. aclu.org/congress/1102301d.html.

38 Barbara Dority, "Your Every Move," *Humanist*, Jan. 2004, p. 14.

39 Thomas Adcock, "Two Projects: One Documents, One Practices 9/11 Pro Bono," N.Y.L.J., Sept. 11, 2002, p. 4.

40 U.S. Const. 6th Amendment.

41 ABA Comm. On BOP-1116, AG Order No. 2529-2001 (2001). Available online. URL: http:// www.abanet.org/poladv/letters/exec/attorneyclient122801.html.

Counterpoint: Immigrants Should Not Have Full Rights to Legal Counsel

1 U.S. Constitution, amendment V; see *Wong Wing v. U.S.* 163 U.S. 228 (1896) (extending Fifth Amendment protections to aliens).

2 Stephen H. Legomsky, "Ten More Years of Plenary Power: Immigration, Congress, and the Courts," 22 HASTINGS CONST. L.Q. 925 (1995).

3 U.S. Constitution, amendment VI.

4 Lininger, "Sects, Lies, and Videotape: The Surveillance and Infiltration of Religious

NOTES

Groups," 89 Iowa L. Rev. 1201, 1274 (2004).

5 Raquel Aldana-Pindell, "The 9/11 'National Security' Cases: Three Principles Guiding Judges' Decision-Making," 81 Or. L. Rev. 985, 994 (2002).

6 Kelly R. Cusick, Note, "Thwarting Ideological Terrorism: Are We Brave Enough to Maintain Civil Liberties in the Face of Terrorist Induced Trauma?", 35 Case W. Res. J. Int'l L. 55, 79 (2003).

7 Michael F. Dowley, Note, "Government Surveillance Powers Under the USA Patriot Act: Is It Possible to Protect National Security and Privacy at the Same Time? A Constitutional Tug-of-War," 36 Suffolk U. L. Rev. 165, 183 (2002).

8 Department of Justice, USA Patriot Act Overview. Available online [pdf]. URL: http://www.lifeandliberty.gov/patriot_overview_pversion.pdf.

9 Paul R. Rice and Benjamin Parlin Saul, "Is the War on Terrorism A War On Attorney-Client Privilege?", 17 Crim. Just. 22, 23 (2002).

10 Ibid.

11 Susan M. Akram and Kevin R. Johnson, "Race, Civil Rights, and Immigration Law After September 11, 2001: The Targeting of Arabs and Muslims," 58 N.Y.U. Ann. Surv. Am. L. 295, 345 (2002).

12 Diana Bellettieri & Khurram Saeed, "What it Means to be a Patriot," J. News, July 4, 2003, p. 1A.

Point: Indefinite Detention of Immigrants Violates Due Process of the Constitution

1 The account of the detention of Turkmen and. Saffi is drawn from the complaint in their class action suit against the U.S. government. Class Action Complaint and Demand For Jury Trial, Turkmen v. Ashcroft (E.D.N.Y. 2002) (No. CV-02-307). Available online [pdf]. URL: http://news.corporate.findlaw.com/hdocs/docs/terrorism/turkmenash41702cmp.pdf.

2 Christopher Drew & Judith Miller, "Though Not Linked to Terrorism, Many Detainees Cannot Go Home," N.Y. Times, Feb. 18, 2002, at A1 (reporting that Justice Department has blocked departure of 87 mostly Arab or Muslim noncitizens who have received voluntary deportation or removal orders "[w]hile investigators comb through information pouring in from overseas to ensure that they have no ties to terrorism").

3 Terry v. Ohio, 392 U.S. 1, 24 (1968).

4 Zadvydas v. Davis, 533 U.S. 678, 701 (2001).

5 An exact number is not available, because on November 5, 2001, when the Justice Department's daily announced running tally was 1147, the Administration responded to criticism about the large number of detainees by abruptly halting its practice of disclosing how many had been detained. It has not released a total figure since that date. See David Cole, "Enemy Aliens," 54 Stan. L. Rev. 953, 960 (2002).

6 Danny Hakim, "4 Are Charged with Belonging to a Terror Cell," N.Y. Times, Aug. 29, 2002, p. A1.

7 All Things Considered (National Public Radio broadcast, Dec. 4, 2001).

8 Office of the Inspector General, U.S. Dept. of Justice, "The September 11 Detainees: A Review of the Treatment of Aliens Held on Immigration Charges in Connection with the Investigation of the September 11 Attacks" (2003).

9 Attorney General's speech to U.S. Conference of Mayors (Oct. 25, 2001).

10 "Attorney General Ashcroft Provides Total Number of Federal Criminal Charges and INS Detainees" (Nov. 27, 2001). Available online. URL: http://www.usdog.gov/ag/speeches/2001/agcrisisremarks11_27.htm.

11 Human Rights Watch, "Presumption of Guilt: Human Rights Abuses of Post-September 11 Detainees," Available online [pdf]. URL: http://www.hrw.org/reports/2002/us911/USA0802.pdf.

12 Ibid., p. 10.

13 Ibid., pp. 60–67.

14 Ibid., p. 67.

15 Ibid., p. 67

16 US Constitution, amends IV,V, XIV.

17 18 USC §3144 provides: Release or detention of material witness: If it appears from an affidavit filed by a partythat the testimony of a person is material in a criminal proceeding and if it is shown that it may become impracticable to

secure the presence of the person by subpoena, a judicial officer may order the arrest of the person and treat the person in accordance with section 3142 of this title. No material witness may be detained because of inability to comply with any condition of release if the testimony of such witness can adequately be secured by deposition, and if further detention is not necessary to prevent a failure of justice. Release of a material witness may be delayed for a reasonable period of time until the deposition of the witness can be taken pursuant to eh Federal Rules of Criminal Procedure.

18 18 USC §3144.

19 *Branzburg v. Hayes,* 408 US 665, 688 (1972).

20 *Costello v. United States,* 350 US 359, 362 (1956).

21 745 F.2d 1250 (9th Cir. 1984).

22 *Lee v. Johnson,* 799 F.2d 31, 36-38 (3d Cir. 1986).

23 483 F.Supp. 1091 (D.Minn. 1979).

24 *United States v. Awadallah,* 202 F. Supp. 2d 55, 78 (2002).

25 Ibid.

26 Brief for Appellee Osama Awadallah filed in the US Court of Appeals for the Second Circuit.

27 *Addington v. Texas,* 441 U.S. 418, 425 (1979).

28 Chang, *Lost Liberties,* p. 64

29 Ibid.

30 Immigrant Rights Clinic, New York University School of Law, New York University Review of Law & Social Change, REVIEW OF LAW & SOCIAL CHANGE, 2000/1, p. 398.

31 Chang, *Lost Liberties,* p. 64.

32 Ibid.

33 Shogren, 2005, p. A24.

Counterpoint: Indefinite Detention of Immigrants Does Not Raise a Constitutional Concern

1 *Fiallo v. Bell,* 430 U.S. 787, 792, (1977).

2 *Mathews v. Diaz,* 426 U.S. 67, 79–80 (1976).

3 *Hamdi v. Rumsfeld,* 542 US 507 (2004).

4 Ibid.

5 Ibid.

6 Ibid.

7 Ibid.

8 *Carlson v. Landon,* 342 U.S. 524, 537 (1952).

9 *Landon v. Plasencia,* 459 U.S. 21, 32-33 (1982).

10 *Al Oduh v United States,* 542 US 466 (2004).

11 "Detainee Cases Making Their Way Through U.S. Federal Courts," Kathleen T. Rhem, American Forces Press Service. Available online. URL: http://www.defenselink.mil/news/newsarticle.aspx?id=31268.

12 *United States v. Awadallah,* 349 F.3d 42 (2d Cir. 2003).

13 *Bacon v. United States,* 449 F.2d 933 (9th Cir. 1971).

14 *United States v. Awadallah.*

Point: There Is a Right of Access to Deportation Hearings in the Wake of 9/11

1 8 USC 1103 (1994).

2 Lord Devlin, "Trial By Jury."

3 Blackstone, Blackstone's *Commentaries on the Laws of England*
Book the Third - Chapter the Twenty-Third: Of the Trial by Jury

4 Michael Cooper, *Dying Behind a Closed Door: Is There a First Amendment Right of Access to Deportation Hearings in the Wake of 9/11?,* p. 5. Available online [pdf]. URL: http://www.ailf.org/awards/dubroff_2003.pdf.

5 8 USC 1229a.

6 Ibid.

7 *Detroit Free Press v. Ashcroft,* 303 F.3d 699–700 (6th Cir. 2002).

8 441 F. Supp 115 (S.D.N.Y. 1977).

9 Ibid., pp. 117–118.

10 8 C.F.R. § § 3.27(b)-(d) (2003).

11 *Press Enterprise Company v. Superior Court of California for Riverside County,* 478 U.S. 1 (1986).

12 Ibid.

13 *Detroit Free Press v. Ashcroft,* 303 F.3d 681, 698-99 (6th Cir. 2002).

14 *Richmond Newspapers, Inc. v. Va.,* 448 U.S. 555, 589 (1980) (Brennan & Marshall, JJ., concurring).

15 *Detroit Free Press v. Ashcroft,* 303 F.3d at 701.

16 Ibid.

17 *Haddad v. Ashcroft,* F. Supp. 2d 799, 803 (E.D. Mich. 2002).

18 *Det. Free Press*, 303 F.3d at 704

**Counterpoint: National Security
Requires That Immigration
Proceedings Be Closed**
1 *The Nation Magazine v. U.S. Deparment
of Defense*, 762 F. Supp. 1558 S.D.N.Y.
(1991).
2 Ibid.
3 *North Jersey Media Group, Inc. v. Ashcroft*,
308 F.3d 198 (3d Cir. 2002), cert denied,
538 U.S. 1056 (2003). Available online.
URL: http://www.ca3.uscourts.gov/opin-
arch/022524.txt.
4 Ibid.

5 Ibid.
6 *Det. Free Press v. Ashcroft*, 303 F.3d 681, 696,
706 (6th Cir. 2002).
7 Ibid.
8 Ibid.
9 Ibid.
10 *North Jersey Media Group, Inc. v. Ashcroft*,
308 F.3d 198, 219 (3d Cir. 2002), cert
denied, 538 U.S. 1056 (2003).
11 Ibid.
12 Ibid.
13 Ibid.
14 Ibid.
15 *Det. Free Press v. Ashcroft*, 303 F.3d 681,
696, 705 (6th Cir. 2002).

RESOURCES ////////

Books and Articles

Aldana-Pindell, Raquel. "The 9/11 'National Security' Cases: Three Principles Guiding Judges' Decision-Making." 81 Or. L. Rev. 985 (2002).

Adock, Thomas. "Two Products: One Document, One Practices 9/11 Pro Bono." N.Y.L.J., Sept 11, 2002.

Cohen, Adam. "Rough Justice," *Time*, Dec. 10, 2001, http://www.time.com/time/magazine/article/0,9171,186641,00.html.

Cole, David. "Enemy Aliens." 54 Stan. L. Rev. 953 (2002).

Conley, Ellen Alexander. *The Chosen Shore: Stories of Immigrants*. Berkeley, Ca.: University of California Press, 2004

Cusick, Kelly. "Thwarting Ideological Terrorism: Are We Brave Enough to Maintain Civil Liberties in the Fact of Terrorist Induced Trauma?" 35 Case W. Res. J. Int'l L. 55 (2003).

Davis, Ann. "Why Detainees Signed Waivers Forfeiting Right to Counsel," *Wall Street Journal*, February 8, 2002.

Dobbins, Teri. "Protecting the Unpopular from the Unreasonable: Warrantless Monitoring of Attorney Client Communications in Federal Prisons." 53 Cath. U. L. Rev, 295 (2004).

Dority, Barbara. "Your Every Move." *Humanist*, January/February 2004.

Drew, Christopher and Judith Miller. "Though Not Linked to Terrorism, Many Detainees Cannot Go Home," *New York Times*, Feb. 18, 2002.

Farnam, Julie. *U.S. Immigration Laws Under the Threat of Terrorism*. New York: Algora Publishing, 2005.

Freeman, Michael. *Freedom or Security : The Consequences for Democracies Using Emergency Powers to Fight Terror*. Westport, Conn.: Praeger Publishers, 2003

Helmer, Gabriel M. "Strip Search and the Felony Detainee: A Case for Reasonable Suspicion." 81 B.U. L. Rev. 239 (2001).

Lininger, Tom. "Sects, Lies, and Videotape: The Surveillance and Infiltration of Religious Groups." 89 Iowa L. Rev. 1201 (2004).

Lee, Erika. *At America's Gates: Chinese Immigration During the Exclusion Era, 1882–1943*. Chapel Hill, N.C.: University of North Carolina Press, 2003.

Legomsky, Stephen. "Ten More Years of Plenary Power: Immigration, Congress, and the Courts." 22 Hastings Const. L.Q. 924 (1995).

Lewis, Thomas T. *The Bill of Rights*. Pasadena, Calif.: Salem Press, 2002

Luchtenberg, Sigrid. *Migration, Education and Change*. London: Routledge Research in Education, 2004.

Lugosi, Charles. "Rule of Law or Rule by Law." 30 Am. J. Crim. L 225 (2003).

Michaels, C. William. *No Greater Threat: America After September 11 and the*

Rise of a National Security State. New York: Algora Publishing, 2002.

Magaña, Lisa. *Straddling the Border : Immigration Policy and the INS*. Austin, Tex.: University of Texas Press, 2003.

Nevins, Joseph. *Operation Gatekeeper : The Rise of the "Illegal Alien" and the Making of the U.S.-Mexico Boundary*. New York: Routledge, 2002.

Rice, Paul and Benjamin Sual. "Is the War on Terrorism a War on Attorney-Client Privilege?" 17 Crim. Jus. 22 (2002).

Tichenor, Daniel J. *Dividing Lines: The Politics of Immigration Control in America*. Princeton, N.J.: Princeton University Press, 2002.

Tsekos, Mary Ellen. "Legislative Focus: Patriot Act." 9 Human Rights Br. 35 (2001).

Whitehead, John W. and Steven Aden. "Forfeiting 'Enduring Freedom' for 'Homeland Security': A Constitutional Analysis of the USA Patriot Act and the Justice Department's Anti-Terrorism Initiatives." 51 Am. U. L. Rev. 1081 (2002).

Web sites

Bureau of Population, Refugees, and Migration (PRM)

http://www.state.gov/g/prm/

PRM has the primary responsibility for formulating policies on population, refugees, and migration, and for administering U.S. refugee assistance and admissions programs. The United States funds protection and relief for millions of refugees and victims of conflict around the globe through the State Department and the PRM is instrumental in this effort.

United States Department of Justice, USA Patriot Overview

http://www.lifeandliberty.gov/patriot_overview_pversion.pdf

The United States Department of Justice has compiled an overview to the USA Patriot Act for ease of understanding.

American Bar Association Commission on Immigration Policy, Practice and Pro Bono

http://www.abanet.org/immigration/

The Commission on Immigration consists of thirteen (13) individuals appointed by the ABA President. The Commission directs Association efforts to ensure fair and unbiased treatment, and full due process rights, for immigrants and refugees within the United States. Acting in coordination with other Association entities, as well as governmental and non-governmental bodies, the Commission

American Civil Liberties Union

http://www.aclu.org

The ACLU is a non-profit organization dedicated to ensuring the Bill of Rights are preserved and guaranteed, including but not limited to preserving the First Amendment, equal protection, due process and privacy.

Center for Immigration Studies

http://www.abanet.org/immigration/

The Center for Immigration Studies is an independent, non-partisan, non-profit research organization. It is the nation's only think tank devoted exclusively to research and policy analysis of the economic, social, demographic, fiscal, and other impacts of immigration on the United States.

Thomas (Legislative Research from the Library of Congress)

http://thomas.loc.gov/

The Library of Congress started the THOMAS research site to make federal legislative resources available at no charge on the internet. The resources available on THOMAS include bill searching, roll call votes, searching legislation by sponsor, the congressional record, the congressional calendar and many more items.

Cases and Statutes

Almeida-Sanchez v. United States, 413 U.S. 266 (1973).
Stated that non-citizens who are facing criminal charges are guaranteed the protections of the Fourth Amendment.

Carlson v. Landon, 342 U.S. 524 (1952).
Held that deporting aliens was subject to procedural due process protections.

Denmore v. Kim, 128 S. Ct. 1708 (2003).
Held that preventative detention of an immigrant awaiting removal proceedings was acceptable.

Detroit Free Press v. Ashcroft, 303 F3d 681 (2002).
Held that the Creppy Directive closing immigration proceedings to the public and press was unconstitutional.

EPA v. Mink, 410 U.S. 73 (1973).
The first Freedom of Information Act case. It held that Congress had not instituted review of documents to judges to determine whether a document was classified or unclassified to determine if it fit into an exception for disclosure. This case was later deemed moot when the FOIA was amended to allow judges to inspect documents to determine their classified nature.

Freedom of Information Act, 5 U.S.C. sec. 552.
The FOIA is a law ensuring public access to U.S. government records.

Pechter v. Lyons, 441 F. Supp. 115 (S.D.N.Y. 1977).
Case established that a judge abused his discretion when he closed an immigration proceeding to the public holding that because there is a liberty interest involved, the public has a right to know.

Rasul v. Bush, 542 U.S. 466 (2004).
Held that the habeas statute, 28 U. S. C. §2241, extends to aliens detained by the United States military overseas, outside the sovereign borders of the United States and beyond the territorial jurisdictions of all its courts.

Richmond Newspapers, Inc. v. Virginia, 448 U.S. 555 (1980).
Established that the was a First Amendment right of access to proceedings. This case also established a test to be used to see if the right existed in the particular proceeding.

Terry v. Ohio, 592 U.S. 1 (1968).
Established that a law enforcement officer may stop a suspect and pat them down for officer safety, without a search warrant.

Upjohn Co. v. United States, 449 U.S. 383 (1981).
Described the attorney-client privilege as the oldest confidential communications known in common law.

The USA PATRIOT Act, Public Law No. 107-56 (2001).
A set of laws, or an act, to deter and punish terrorist acts in the United States and

around the world, to enhance law enforcement investigatory tools, and for other purposes.

Yamataya v. Fisher, 189 U.S. 86 (1903).
Stated that non-citizens were protected under the Due Process clause of the Fifth Amendment.

Zadvydas v. Davis, 533 U.S. 678 (2001).
Established that the Due Process clause of the United States Constitution applies to all persons in the United States, including aliens, legal or illegal.

Terms and Concepts

alien
civil rights
deportation
due process
habeas corpus
in camera
liberty
Miranda rights
privileged communication
removal

APPENDIX

Beginning Legal Research

The goal of POINT/COUNTERPOINT is not only to provide the reader with an introduction to a controversial issue affecting society, but also to encourage the reader to explore the issue more fully. This appendix, then, is meant to serve as a guide to the reader in researching the current state of the law as well as exploring some of the public-policy arguments as to why existing laws should be changed or new laws are needed.

Like many types of research, legal research has become much faster and more accessible with the invention of the Internet. This appendix discusses some of the best starting points, but of course "surfing the Net" will uncover endless additional sources of information—some more reliable than others. Some important sources of law are not yet available on the Internet, but these can generally be found at the larger public and university libraries. Librarians usually are happy to point patrons in the right direction.

The most important source of law in the United States is the Constitution. Originally enacted in 1787, the Constitution outlines the structure of our federal government and sets limits on the types of laws that the federal government and state governments can pass. Through the centuries, a number of amendments have been added to or changed in the Constitution, most notably the first ten amendments, known collectively as the Bill of Rights, which guarantee important civil liberties. Each state also has its own constitution, many of which are similar to the U.S. Constitution. It is important to be familiar with the U.S. Constitution because so many of our laws are affected by its requirements. State constitutions often provide protections of individual rights that are even stronger than those set forth in the U.S. Constitution.

Within the guidelines of the U.S. Constitution, Congress—both the House of Representatives and the Senate—passes bills that are either vetoed or signed into law by the President. After the passage of the law, it becomes part of the United States Code, which is the official compilation of federal laws. The state legislatures use a similar process, in which bills become law when signed by the state's governor. Each state has its own official set of laws, some of which are published by the state and some of which are published by commercial publishers. The U.S. Code and the state codes are an important source of legal research; generally, legislators make efforts to make the language of the law as clear as possible.

However, reading the text of a federal or state law generally provides only part of the picture. In the American system of government, after the

101

legislature passes laws and the executive (U.S. President or state governor) signs them, it is up to the judicial branch of the government, the court system, to interpret the laws and decide whether they violate any provision of the Constitution. At the state level, each state's supreme court has the ultimate authority in determining what a law means and whether or not it violates the state constitution. However, the federal courts—headed by the U.S. Supreme Court—can review state laws and court decisions to determine whether they violate federal laws or the U.S. Constitution. For example, a state court may find that a particular criminal law is valid under the state's constitution, but a federal court may then review the state court's decision and determine that the law is invalid under the U.S. Constitution.

It is important, then, to read court decisions when doing legal research. The Constitution uses language that is intentionally very general—for example, prohibiting "unreasonable searches and seizures" by the police—and court cases often provide more guidance. For example, the U.S. Supreme Court's 2001 decision in *Kyllo* v. *United States* held that scanning the outside of a person's house using a heat sensor to determine whether the person is growing marijuana is unreasonable—*if* it is done without a search warrant secured from a judge. Supreme Court decisions provide the most definitive explanation of the law of the land, and it is therefore important to include these in research. Often, when the Supreme Court has not decided a case on a particular issue, a decision by a federal appeals court or a state supreme court can provide guidance; but just as laws and constitutions can vary from state to state, so can federal courts be split on a particular interpretation of federal law or the U.S. Constitution. For example, federal appeals courts in Louisiana and California may reach opposite conclusions in similar cases.

Lawyers and courts refer to statutes and court decisions through a formal system of citations. Use of these citations reveals which court made the decision (or which legislature passed the statute) and when and enables the reader to locate the statute or court case quickly in a law library. For example, the legendary Supreme Court case *Brown* v. *Board of Education* has the legal citation 347 U.S. 483 (1954). At a law library, this 1954 decision can be found on page 483 of volume 347 of the U.S. Reports, the official collection of the Supreme Court's decisions. Citations can also be helpful in locating court cases on the Internet.

Understanding the current state of the law leads only to a partial understanding of the issues covered by the POINT/COUNTERPOINT series. For a fuller understanding of the issues, it is necessary to look at public-policy arguments that the current state of the law is not adequately addressing the issue.

Many groups lobby for new legislation or changes to existing legislation; the National Rifle Association (NRA), for example, lobbies Congress and the state legislatures constantly to make existing gun control laws less restrictive and not to pass additional laws. The NRA and other groups dedicated to various causes might also intervene in pending court cases: a group such as Planned Parenthood might file a brief *amicus curiae* (as "a friend of the court")—called an "amicus brief"—in a lawsuit that could affect abortion rights. Interest groups also use the media to influence public opinion, issuing press releases and frequently appearing in interviews on news programs and talk shows. The books in POINT/COUNTERPOINT list some of the interest groups that are active in the issue at hand, but in each case there are countless other groups working at the local, state, and national levels. It is important to read everything with a critical eye, for sometimes interest groups present information in a way that can be read only to their advantage. The informed reader must always look for bias.

Finding sources of legal information on the Internet is relatively simple thanks to "portal" sites such as FindLaw (*www.findlaw.com*), which provides access to a variety of constitutions, statutes, court opinions, law review articles, news articles, and other resources—including all Supreme Court decisions issued since 1893. Other useful sources of information include the U.S. Government Printing Office (*www.gpo.gov*), which contains a complete copy of the U.S. Code, and the Library of Congress's THOMAS system (*thomas.loc.gov*), which offers access to bills pending before Congress as well as recently passed laws. Of course, the Internet changes every second of every day, so it is best to do some independent searching. Most cases, studies, and opinions that are cited or referred to in public debate can be found online—and *everything* can be found in one library or another.

The Internet can provide a basic understanding of most important legal issues, but not all sources can be found there. To find some documents it is necessary to visit the law library of a university or a public law library; some cities have public law libraries, and many library systems keep legal documents at the main branch. On the following page are some common citation forms.

COMMON CITATION FORMS

Source of Law	Sample Citation	Notes
U.S. Supreme Court	*Employment Division v. Smith,* 485 U.S. 660 (1988)	The U.S. Reports is the official record of Supreme Court decisions. There is also an unofficial Supreme Court ("S. Ct.") reporter.
U.S. Court of Appeals	*United States v. Lambert,* 695 F.2d 536 (11th Cir.1983)	Appellate cases appear in the Federal Reporter, designated by "F." The 11th Circuit has jurisdiction in Alabama, Florida, and Georgia.
U.S. District Court	*Carillon Importers, Ltd. v. Frank Pesce Group, Inc.,* 913 F.Supp. 1559 (S.D.Fla.1996)	Federal trial-level decisions are reported in the Federal Supplement ("F. Supp."). Some states have multiple federal districts; this case originated in the Southern District of Florida.
U.S. Code	Thomas Jefferson Commemoration Commission Act, 36 U.S.C., §149 (2002)	Sometimes the popular names of legislation—names with which the public may be familiar—are included with the U.S. Code citation.
State Supreme Court	*Sterling v. Cupp,* 290 Ore. 611, 614, 625 P.2d 123, 126 (1981)	The Oregon Supreme Court decision is reported in both the state's reporter and the Pacific regional reporter.
State Statute	Pennsylvania Abortion Control Act of 1982, 18 Pa. Cons. Stat. 3203-3220 (1990)	States use many different citation formats for their statutes.

PICTURE CREDITS

WENDY E. BIDDLE, J.D., is a native of Michigan and currently resides in Minnesota. She attended Western Michigan University where she majored in Political Science. Wendy graduated from Valparaiso University School of Law where she was an executive member of the Valparaiso Law Review. While a member of the *Review* she published an article analyzing statutory interpretation. Ms. Biddle is pursuing a Master's in Library and Information Science at the University of Pittsburgh to add to her repertoire. Her main interests in research and writing are civil rights, immigration, statutory interpretation and technology law. Aside from writing, Wendy enjoys photography and art.

ALAN MARZILLI, M.A., J.D., lives in Washington, D.C., and is a program associate with Advocates for Human Potential, Inc., a research and consulting firm based in Sudbury, MA, and Albany, NY. He primarily works on developing training and educational materials for agencies of the Federal government on topics such as housing, mental health policy, employment, and transportation. He has spoken on mental health issues in thirty states, the District of Columbia, and Puerto Rico; his work has included training mental health administrators, nonprofit management and staff, and people with mental illnesses and their families on a wide variety of topics, including effective advocacy, community-based mental health services, and housing. He has written several handbooks and training curricula that are used nationally—as far away as the territory of Guam. He managed statewide and national mental health advocacy programs and worked for several public interest lobbying organizations while studying law at Georgetown University. He has written more than a dozen books, including numerous titles in the *Point/Counterpoint* series.